IMAGES
OF
OUR TRUE DESTINY

By

Howard H. Robertson, M.D.

PublishAmerica

Baltimore

ISBN: 1-4241-1777-1
PUBLISHED BY PUBLISHAMERICA, LLLP
www.publishamerica.com
Baltimore

Printed in the United States of America

Dedicated to

My Greatest Cheerleader,

My Wife,

Jami

TABLE OF CONTENTS

INTRODUCTION

The philosophers in ancient times taught that the world was the center of the universe. Man was the most sublime creation of the Gods and everything in the universe was created for man's benefit. In modern times science shows that earth is just an ordinary planet orbiting an average star. It demonstrates that the universe contains billions of similar stars and humans are complex animals struggling for survival. For the past several hundred years there is a wide divergence between religious teachings and the discoveries of science. There are also many differing philosophical and religious doctrines being currently followed throughout the world. The world is filled with ideas and theories which attempt to explain the universe and the role of humanity. There is a yearning for truth within each of us, a desire to know about the universe and our place within it. Each of us must decide for ourselves what to believe. We each must decide who we are and how we relate to the universe.

I am a medical doctor by profession and over the years I have had many encounters with the healing process that could not be easily explained by current scientific theories. I have had spiritual experiences where I believe I was touched by the hand of God. These experiences have led me to ask many questions, such as: Does God exist? Who am I really? What is my relationship to God? Why was the universe created? Was it created, or did it just happen? Who is really in charge here? What am I doing here? Why am I alive?

The resolution of these types of questions has led me on a lifelong search for meaning in my life. It is surprising to me that the more I learn, the more life tries to teach me. Just when I think I have a good handle on the reality of life and I am comfortable with the truths that I understand, the events of my life shake me, challenge me, and lead me to search out new meaning and direction. I now see images of truth everywhere I look. I often feel we are like the blind men trying to describe an elephant, each one taking hold of a different part of its body and arguing that the whole elephant is like that body part.

The Blind Men and The Elephant
by John Godfrey Saxe (1816-1887)

"It was six men of Indostan
To learning much inclined,
Who went to see the Elephant
    (Though all of them were blind),
That each by observation
    Might satisfy his mind.

The First approached the Elephant,
    And happening to fall
Against his broad and sturdy side,
    At once began to bawl:
"God bless me! But the Elephant
    Is very like a WALL!"

The Second, feeling of the tusk,
Cried, "Ho! What have we here
So very round and smooth and sharp?
    To me 'tis mighty clear
This wonder of an Elephant

Is very like a SPEAR!"

The Third approached the animal,
        And happening to take
The squirming trunk within his hands,
        Thus boldly up and spake:
"I see," quoth he, "the Elephant
        Is very like a SNAKE!"

The Fourth reached out an eager hand,
        And felt about the knee
"What most this wondrous beast is like
        Is mighty plain, "quoth he:
""Tis clear enough the Elephant
        Is very like a TREE!"

The Fifth, who chanced to touch the ear,
        Said: "E'en the blindest man
Can tell what this resembles most;
        Deny the fact who can,
This marvel of an Elephant
        Is very like a FAN!"

The Sixth no sooner had begun
        About the beast to grope,
Than seizing on the swinging tail
        That fell within his scope,
"I see," quoth he, "the Elephant
        Is very like a ROPE!"

And so these men of Indostan
        Disputed loud and long,

Each in his own opinion
Exceeding stiff and strong,
Though each was partly in the right,
And all were in the wrong!

There is a very wide diversity of opinion about the reality of our existence. It appears that every person and every religion has its own version of cosmic truth. I believe through my own personal prayer, study, meditation, and inspiration that we have much more in common with each other than differences. I feel like my blind eyes are being opened and that I am beginning to see the elephant as a whole. Often, we are describing different aspects of reality, or using analogy to illustrate difficult concepts. We should be celebrating our common beliefs instead of fighting over our differences.

This book contains my opinions. It does not represent one religion except my personal religion. It is true that I consider myself a Christian, because I believe that Jesus Christ is my personal savior, the Savior of all mankind, and I believe very much in the truths taught in the Old and New Testaments, but I accept the teachings of all religions that resonate with me and feel truthful. The Spirit of God helps all people to recognize truth, inspires you and me, and works in all people who are earnestly seeking to find truth. I am often surprised and delighted to find many common ideas and teachings basic to many divergent religious persuasions, both ancient and modern. I hope that some of the things I write in this book will resonate with you and will encourage you to seek for a closer relationship with God.

The understanding that we create our own destiny and thereby the world in which we live is a critical message that needs to permeate every human mind. We need to start consciously choosing what kind of world we desire to create instead of unconsciously creating our current world of chaos and strife. Humanity needs to advance its collective consciousness into an era of harmony and wisdom. We have acted like spoiled children expecting someone else to fix our problems. It is time to grow up, mature, and be responsible for ourselves and the world around us.

I hope that this book will help inspire people to live in greater peace and harmony one with another. In writing these things I desire to help everyone to progress spiritually and to be more tolerant of others and their beliefs. We live in a world bent on self destruction and it is critical at this time for humanity to start working together to solve the problems which face us all. We can no longer waste precious resources in fighting among ourselves over our personal beliefs.

This book begins with a description of basic beliefs concerning who we are, why we are here, and where we are headed because beliefs are the basis of creation. What we believe determines how we feel, think, and act. A better understanding of who we are is essential to improvement in our personal lives and the world as a whole.

This is followed by a discussion of basic eternal truths. These truths are tools that we all have for use in shaping our lives. We have the ability to use universal laws consciously or unconsciously. It is far better to be aware of these laws in order to plan and direct our lives in the manner we desire. It is up to each one of us to use these laws to our advantage and to solve the problems which we each face. Awareness, understanding, and implementation of these laws are the best ways to heal our own life and the world around us.

The final part of this book is a plea to work together to resolve conflict and to create a life of joy, love, and peace. We can improve the world, but we must look to ourselves for the strength and motivation to improve ourselves first. The answers to our personal situation come from within. The answers to our world situation come from within each of us personally.

CHAPTER I
WHO AM I?

1. Eternal Being

The truth is that we are eternal. We have always existed. We will always exist. You are not really your body. I am not my body. We are eternal souls who exist independent of our bodies. Our bodies are just part of this current reality of earth life, allowing us to experience physical sensations. Our consciousness existed before we were born and we will continue after our death.

Earlier in my life I was fascinated with near death experiences and read several books on the phenomenon. As a physician I had a few patients tell me about their out of body perceptions when they had a brush with near death. It was during my mid life that I met and married my current spouse, Jami. She related to me her personal experience with near death. When she was fourteen years old she went for a drive with her best friend, Julie, who had just turned seventeen and had recently received her driver's license. They were living in the mountains of northern Arizona and went to explore one of the scenic roads in Oak Creek Canyon between Flagstaff and Sedona. It was Mother's day, a beautiful spring day with sunshine, gentle breezes, and flowing water. The road was narrow and twisted as it wound down into the canyon. Julie drove too fast for the conditions. In her youthful exuberance she overestimated her ability to control the car, and underestimated the treacherous curves ahead. Jami was frightened, she felt that Julie was out of control, but she was too afraid to even cry out to tell Julie to slow down. The car ran off the road, rolled over and over a total of eight times, and the girls were flung out of the car. Julie was found with her neck and head resting on top of a road sign, dead. Jami was pinned between the car and a fence, unconscious, her pulse and heartbeat weak. While the paramedics and police worked to free and stabilize her, Jami's heart stopped and it was shocked back into beating successfully.

Jami remembers very little of the actual accident. She remembers smacking the dashboard with her head and then leaving her body behind. She floated up into the tree tops and watched as the car rolled over and over beneath her in slow motion. She journeyed up into a bright area where she was lying down on her back and she was surrounded by bright light. There was a being there who was bright and radiant. When she met the being, Jami saw it was a lady, dressed all in white, who held her and stroked Jami's hair, comforting her. The lady told Jami not to be afraid, that everything would be all right. Jami closed her eyes, and when she opened them again, she was in the ambulance being taken to the hospital. Jami felt no pain during the accident. She felt joy and comfort in the presence of the woman in white. Her pain only began when she was back in her body struggling with the healing process. Jami knows that there is life after death and that we exist outside of this earth experience.

When we think of our identity we have to realize that we are really not our body. If someone loses a leg, for instance, they do not suddenly stop existing. Even substantial damage to the brain often leaves the personality of the injured person relatively intact. As we age we often feel much different than what our body appears. In my forties I felt much like I did as when I was twenty. I am sometimes surprised when my body does not respond to my desires like it used to when I was younger. I do not consciously feel much different; my personal identity has not really changed much over the years. I certainly understand more and I have more learning and knowledge just as I have more responsibilities, yet my personal identity has not changed much over the years. I still like and dislike many of the same foods, smells, and activities of years past. My basic personality and outlook on life has not changed.

The truth that we are eternal creatures says that we have no beginning and no end. We have always existed. This is a very hard concept for many people. The idea of eternity is so foreign to us here in this physical experience. On this earth everything has a beginning and an end. Birth and death, the cycles of life, this is what we all see around us every day. It is part of our earthly experience. To have no birth and to have no death is incomprehensible.

The world we live in blinds us to the truth of our eternal nature. It is a camouflage that veils our minds from the eternal realms. Everything we see around us has a beginning and an end. The dimensions of space and time set up conditions which hide other dimensions and the idea of no time. Many of the basic assumptions we have about our nature and the nature of our world are just illusions. We think we are our body, but our body is just the projection of our spiritual selves into this reality. We think time is real, when it is again, just an illusion.

Many scientist working with quantum physics have shown that time and space are not as solid or static as they seem. Matter is mostly empty space, an illusion of solidity. Everything is made up of vibrating energy and everything has a certain innate intelligence of its own. Our world is like a hologram, it appears solid and dimensional yet it is just a projection of energy. Our interpretation of our world is only what our minds interpret from the electrical signals sent to it from the sensory organs, eyes, ears, taste, touch, and smell.

Time is also an illusion. Its quality changes dramatically depending on what we are doing. It passes very quickly when we are intently engaged in a pleasurable experience. It slows down when we dislike or are bored with our situation. Minutes waiting in line seem like hours and hours vacationing seem like minutes. Space, time, and this earth life are illusions which are created to allow us our independent experience. The truth about our nature is difficult, yet beautiful and simple. We are eternal creatures, progressing throughout the ages. This Earth is just a way station for us to visit for a time before going forward on our eternal journey.

Imagine you are on a long journey. It is so long that you really cannot remember where or when it started, you have been traveling on a train ever since you could remember. There are train stops along the way. At each stop some people get on and some get off. We do not know much about the details, for instance, we do not know how many stops there are along the way, or if someone can get off at the same stop more than once. We do know that everyone is on the same journey and that we are all traveling together. This earth life is just one of the stops along the way. It is an important stop, but it is just one of the many stops along our eternal journey. We do not begin our existence at birth; our existence will not end when we die. Knowing and believing that we are eternal creatures is essential to understanding our role in the universe and our purpose here on earth.

Believing that we are eternal beings allows us to relax a little and realize that everything is going to be alright. Nothing in this earthly reality can really harm us in any way. It is all a temporary illusion. It is alright to enjoy what life brings, we can trust ourselves. We have existed for eons and we are wiser and stronger than we realize. I believe that within each of us are all the tools and knowledge necessary to solve any problem we face. We each need to trust our own consciousness and act in the manner that feels right for us.

A belief in our eternal nature also instills in us a greater need to love and respect those around us. Can you imagine having harmed someone here on earth, only to find out later that they were our best friend in the eternities? This is one reason why Christ taught us to love others as ourselves. The irritating customer in this life may be an eternal friend and we would be embarrassed in the eternities if we treat them poorly now. I try to act in a way that I do not feel like I have to lie about my actions. If I am so embarrassed about my actions now that I want to lie about them and hide them, then think how embarrassed I will be later when everyone knows what I did or thought. People lie and deceive others because they think they can get away with it. Knowing that we are all eternal beings reminds us that no one really gets away with anything. If we want to avoid suffering and embarrassment in this life or future lives, it is wise to treat ourselves and others well. Do unto others as you would have others do to you.

2. Child of God

We are often told that we are all God's children. When I talk to people about what this means to them I am informed that "God created us" or that God thought of us and brought us into being. I have often wondered what this really means. How are we different from any of God's other creations? How are we different from the other mammals that walk this earth or the trees and rocks that make up the earth? If we are eternal beings then how could we be created by God?

I believe our intelligence or our ability to learn, progress, and develop has always existed, it is eternal and it is of the same nature as God. This is the spark of true divinity which is at the core of each of us. It cannot be made or unmade, but is eternal. Our ability to learn is the basic part of us that has no beginning and has no end.

We are children of God because God took some of the eternal intelligence that has always existed and then formed it into spiritual immortal bodies, forming our individual spirits. Our spirits are created in a way similar to the creation of stars. Stars are created when the gasses floating in the universe are gathered together until they ignite and shine forth. Our spirits are made from the gathering together of eternal intelligence until consciousness develops. Each of us is different from one another, just as each star is different from another. We are unique individuals, created from the eternal intelligence which has always existed. This birthing process has been described recently as sparks being thrown off of a great mass of intelligence and each spark is formed into a spirit body. These newly created spirits are seen as immature forms which slowly grow in the spirit dimension. We learn and develop there until we progress to the point that we desire this earthly experience. Our spirit body will never die and will never cease to be. At our earthly birth our spirit is then joined with our physical bodies to produce our current selves. Our body is controlled by our spirit like a puppet on a string. This body is a vehicle for our earthly reality.

Our physical, earthly body is created by our earthly parents and our spiritual body is created by our heavenly parents. Both Heavenly Father and Heavenly Mother are described by ancient and modern religions and by contemporary spiritual psychics. Both are revered as Deity. We literally are sons and daughters of our spiritual heavenly parents. Our spiritual bodies allowed our intelligence to learn, grow, and progress in the spiritual dimensions, just like our physical body allows further experience, growth and progression in our earthly dimension. We are on an eternal mission to grow and develop and become one with our Heavenly Parents.

This family analogy is given to help us understand our relationship with God. In truth our eternal reality is impossible to fully describe in our current language and physical understanding. It is more like we are waves in the ocean and God is the ocean. We are one with God. We are more like God than we can possibly suspect. When Jesus Christ walked on earth He demonstrated that we as humans are much more capable than most of us realize.

The knowledge that we are all brothers and sisters together here on earth should encourage us to treat each other in a loving manner. When children are young they often fight and squabble with one another due to their own selfish immature desires and jealousies. As adults these petty childhood differences usually fall away and adult siblings are often good friends. It is time for the human race to grow up and stop acting like spoiled children. We are able to love one another and get along well with each other here on earth. We are all family. We are all one.

3. One with God

When we look around at each other in this world we perceive ourselves as separate from others. We think and believe each person on earth to be individual, isolated, and unconnected from every other person. Religions teach that because of the fall of Adam we humans are separated from God and that the great work to be done here on earth is to become reconnected with God's spirit. Many of the conflicts of mankind have been due to the idea that one group is separate from another and needs to fight for survival. Religious groups often emphasize our differences and try to make everyone conform to one ideal.

I think that this perception of individuality is an illusion of this earthly state and that we are actually very connected to each other. When Christ taught that He and The Father are one, and Christ wanted all mankind to be one with them, He suggested that we are more connected to each other than we know. We are all one. We are connected with each other and we are connected with God. We are like the cells that make up the human body that may be very different from each other, but all are part of the body. All are individual, unique cells but joined together in one functioning organism. We may all be different, but we are all connected to each other and make up the body of humanity.

Our connection is more than just spiritual; it is a physical reality of this world. The electrical activity of our bodies, our thoughts, the movements of our muscles, the impulses of our nerves all radiate outward from us. This electrical activity produces an electromagnetic field much like a radio signal emanating from our bodies. It is strongest right next to our body and may be easily measured electrically, such as with EEG and EKG recordings. The ability to measure the electrical signals of the brain has allowed researchers to determine that young infants feel emotions, such as empathy, anger, and jealousy. Some people can see this field close to the body and have named it our aura.

This aura, or electrical field, spreads out into the universe like radio waves from a broadcast or light from the sun. The further away it spreads, the weaker it becomes, but it still is present. We respond to the electrical signals of those around us, we can pick up on other people's feelings when we are close to them. We have all had the experience of entering a room during an argument and feeling the tension in the air, or feeling depressed ourselves when attending someone who is very ill or depressed themselves. All of our fields mix and cross and intermingle. Our thoughts and actions ripple through humanity and the entire universe. We affect others and others affect us. We are all one and connected electrically and spiritually with one another.

Many of us believe that our thoughts are private. They are not. Every second we broadcast our thoughts like radio signals throughout the cosmos. They are easily known and experienced in other dimensions. The universe responds to our thoughts. Our thinking affects us, those around us, the worldly environment, and the eternal realms.

God's spirit permeates all of us and the entire universe. We are all part of that spiritual field. We are all part of God and God is in all of us. Separation is an illusion. We are in God's presence at every moment throughout our lives. We could no more be separated from God than we could be separated from ourselves.

We are children of God who are one with each other and one with God. We are all progressing to become like God. We are following in the footsteps of Jesus Christ who has already become perfected and deified with the Father. We are eternal beings progressing throughout the eternities.

The belief that we are all one and we are one with God changes our perspective enormously. We literally treat God the way we treat a stranger that we meet. We literally love ourselves when we love our neighbor. When we help someone else we are really helping our self. When we are happy God is happy.

CHAPTER II
WHY AM I HERE?

1. Gain Body

This earth life is a special school of learning for our souls. We are in an important stage of our personal progression towards perfection. The purposes for being here on earth in this mortal experience are multiple, but all are critical for our eternal development.

We separated ourselves from the presence of God to come to earth and experience this physical reality. It is important to experience a body. When we were undifferentiated intelligence our ability to have personal learning experiences was very limited. Our organization into spirit bodies, performed for us by God, gave us the ability to learn and progress. This earthly experience with its physical reality allows us to learn and grow in important ways also. We chose to leave God and journey here in this earthly realm for the chance to learn and grow. It is supposed to be a joyful experience. We were not kicked out of God's presence because we are bad. We left because we were good enough to have creative experiences outside of God's dimension.

The idea that we chose to come to earth is often hard for people to believe because much of our personal limitations, suffering, and poor choices have come about precisely because of our physical needs. It often appears better to them to be just a spirit living in heaven with other spirits; one with God, pure energy that never gets sick or injured, never needs to eat or sleep. Many of the world's religions felt the same way, teaching that the body is corrupt and naturally evil and that in order to get closer to God and gain personal spirituality we had to deny the needs of the body through severely limiting or denying our physical inclinations. The principles of fasting, sexual abstinence, refraining from singing or dancing all derive from the idea that the body is evil.

The body is not evil. We are allowed to be here to have additional experiences which would be impossible without being in this physical realm. Physical pleasure and pain are earthly experiences. All of the activities relating to maintaining our bodies and reproducing are limited to this physical realm and are very educational for us. Learning to solve our own problems and to truly love others can only come when we act as individuals. We do not have to give up anything physical to be able to grow spiritually. It might be easier to remain a spirit and many of our siblings might make that choice. We chose to come to earth to learn and grow further. We decided to go off to college to get advanced training.

Owning a car is not bad just because people often get hurt or killed when it is not operated correctly. Most people find that having a car is very beneficial and helps with one's ability to get from one place to another. Many people choose to own and use cars. Before a person receives the privilege of driving a car they are taught how to drive safely. A training program for driving is important prior to gaining a driver's license. If someone keeps driving in a dangerous manner, harming others, or using poor judgment with the operation of the car, he loses his license to drive and has to hang up his car keys.

I believe that the same is true with a body. It can be a dangerous thing for our spirits to operate. I think that God allowed us to come to this environment to have a beginner body to learn to control. It is true that in this driving school for the body there are poor choices, dangerous maneuvers, and many people really mess up. We are allowed to have a full range of experience. However, there is nothing that we can do here in this earth plane that will harm our true selves, even dying just returns us to the spiritual dimension where we may review our life, learn from our mistakes, and feel the joy and love of God. Many people believe that we get sent back to earth in another body to try again. Eventually, most of us as we age and mature learn how to control the body effectively and are able to concentrate more on the needs of the spirit rather than the urges of the body. If we are ever going to progress and become like the resurrected Christ, it would be important to learn how to be like Christ in a safe (safe for our true selves) environment.

I personally believe in a physical resurrection, that we will all eventually be able to project a physical manifestation or body whenever desired in any appropriate dimensional reality. Many Christians believe that the resurrection of Christ was a spiritual manifestation which represents our spiritual immortality and do not believe that the resurrection was and is literal. The Bible plainly teaches of the physical resurrection.

In the Old Testament the vision of the resurrection by Ezekiel clearly is talking about a physical reconstruction of our bodies. "The power of the LORD was upon me and I was carried away by the spirit of the LORD to a valley full of old, dry bones that were scattered everywhere across the ground. He led me around among them, and then He said unto me: "Son of dust, can these bones become people again?"

I replied, "Lord, you alone know the answer to that."

Then he told me to speak to the bones and say: "O dry bones, listen to the words of God, for the Lord God says, See! I am going to make you live and breathe again! I will replace the flesh and muscles on you and cover you with skin. I will put breath into you, and you shall live and know I am the Lord."

So I spoke these words from God, just as he told me to; and suddenly there was a rattling noise from all across the valley, and the bones of each body came together and attached to each other as they used to be. Then, as I watched, the muscles and flesh formed over the bones, and skin covered them, but the bodies had no breath. Then he told me to call to the wind and say: "The Lord God says: Come from the four winds, O Spirit, and breathe upon these slain bodies, that they may live again." So I spoke to the winds as he commanded me and the bodies began breathing; they lived, and stood up—a very great army." (Ezekiel 37:1-10)

In the New Testament, Christ is obviously a physical being after His resurrection, with adoring disciples touching Him and eating with Him. The book of Luke states, "…Jesus himself was suddenly standing there among them, and greeted them. But the whole group was terribly frightened, thinking they were seeing a ghost!

"Why are you frightened?" he asked. "Why do you doubt that it is really I? Look at my hands! Look at my feet! You can see that it is I, myself! Touch me and make sure that I am not a ghost! For ghosts don't have bodies, as you see that I do!" As he spoke, he held out his hands for them to see the marks of the nails, and showed them the wounds in his feet.

Still they stood there undecided, filled with joy and doubt.

Then he asked them, "Do you have anything here to eat?"

They gave him a piece of broiled fish, and he ate it as they watched." (Luke 24:36-43)

I believe that we, like Christ, will resurrect and have our spiritual selves and our physical selves all merged together in an immortal being. I echo the belief expressed by Job, "But as for me, I know that my Redeemer lives, and that he will stand upon the earth at last. And I know that after this body has decayed, this body shall see God!" (Job 19:25-26)

We have to realize that it is not really about our bodies. People often place way too much emphasize on our bodies and what we can and cannot do. The body is really unimportant; it is the experience that we seek. It is how we think and view life that matters. It is how we develop our creativity and how much we love that really counts. We may even develop other types of bodies and abilities in future eternal realms to allow us to further progress. Eternity is a long time and I am sure that we cannot conceive everything about it from our earthly perspective.

2. Experience in Safe Environment

The experiences we have during our life are important to our learning and add to our wisdom and progression. The skills needed to progress in the eternities cannot be given by another, but may only be developed by the individual. God will not force anyone to heaven, because He cannot. The nature of perfection has to come from within, a habit of loving. Just like it is impossible to learn to play a violin well by reading about it, studying about it, and listening to others play. A violinist has to pick up the violin and practice to become proficient at playing well. There are very few skills that can be taught to someone without them practicing the skill. I would rather have a welder with twenty years experience than a welder that has read and studied welding for twenty years. Physicians do a better job after they have practiced their profession for a while, which is why medical schools have two years of book work and two years of patient care, followed by internship and residency experience for a few more years prior to licensing.

Humans are in training to be perfected. We have to practice the skills necessary in order to progress. God gives us great ability and it is our responsibility to develop our talents and learn to love others. There is a learning curve that has to take place. We can choose the easy way or the hard way. Some of our actions will bring us misery and others will lead to joy. We are allowed to learn at our own pace, and God will never interfere with the learning process. He may teach, love, and encourage, but He will never prevent the natural consequences of our beliefs and choices, no matter how painful those consequences may be. We have true freedom of choice. Earth is a safe place that God has provided to us to learn and gain experience without injuring our true selves. It is better to make mistakes and errors in judgment here on earth where the damage is limited to life on earth than it would to make mistakes in the eternal realms where we might damage whole galaxies. Some people believe that we have the opportunity to return to earth over and over again until we get it right.

We are here to gain experience for ourselves to distinguish between what is good and bad, what works and what does not. We all have choices to make every second of every day. We choose what to wear, when to bathe, what to eat, even what to think. There is nothing that happens to us about which we do not have to make a decision. Some decisions we make once, others we end up making over and over again. In my youth I decided that I would not smoke cigarettes. I thought that they stank. I could not imagine sucking on those nasty stinking objects. I have not had to make that decision over and over again, when offered a cigarette I automatically say, "No thanks, I do not smoke." And that is that. It is automatic, I do not even think about it. As a doctor I never even questioned the need to go into work and keep my appointments for the day. I just got up out of bed in the morning and went. It was automatic. The alarm went off and I was up. Now I have to decide every day whether to get up or not. My body hurts a great amount and lying in my warm comfortable bed provides for the least amount of pain. I have to decide how much pain I have in relation to how important my daily tasks seem to determine how long I may linger in comfort. I have seen the direct consequences of some of my choices in life and have regrets that I did not have enough wisdom at the time to make better choices. Most of my choices are not truly good versus evil, but what works and what does not work, what brings peace and happiness versus what brings conflict and disappointment.

There was a youth who asked the elderly sage how he could gain wisdom and make wise choices. The sage answered, "Through experience." When asked how to gain experience the sage answered, "Through poor choices." At age fifty, I know more than I did at age twenty. Think about how much more I will know at age eighty. I certainly value my father's opinion now much more than I did in my youth.

Adam and Eve left God's presence for tasting the fruit of the "Tree of Knowledge of Good and Evil". They were sent to this earthly dimension so that they could experience life and learn from their own efforts what works and what does not. The story of Adam and Eve is an analogy of our own lives. We likewise have left the spiritual dimension to sojourn here in this earthly reality for exactly the same purpose, to learn from our personal experience.

We are not sent here alone, we have been given a lot of guidance and counsel from God. He has sent his advice forth upon the earth in every age and in every nation of the world. The Bible, The Torah, The Qu'aran, The Bhagavad Ghita, The Book of Mormon are all examples of books written by people inspired by God for the dissemination of spiritual information. Some people look quickly to help and advice from these sources and those they feel are wiser and more knowledgeable than they. Others insist on trying things out for themselves for personal experience. God has left keys of knowledge, signposts of help, and clues to show us our path in life. We may choose to use the knowledge already present, or we may choose to ignore it. But when we do not use what we already are given, why would the Lord give us more? In every age of man, in every part of the world, when people are looking to God for inspiration and guidance, revelation abounds. God is no respecter of persons. It does not really matter what church you currently attend or what land you live in, if you desire wisdom from God, and pursue spiritual matters, God will respond and communicate with you.

The New Testament teaches, "If you want to know what God wants you to do, ask him, and he will gladly tell you, for he is always ready to give a bountiful supply of wisdom to all who ask him; he will not resent it. But when you ask him, be sure that you really expect him to tell you, for a doubtful mind will be as unsettled as a wave of the sea that is driven and tossed by the wind;" (James 1:5-6)

Everyone has the same connection with God. We are all one and one with God. No one has any greater right to personal inspiration from God than anyone else. We do not need to go through any mortal to gain access to God's spirit and grace. Not Mary nor Moses nor Abraham nor Mohammed nor any other person. God communicates with each one of us on a daily basis. It is up to us to learn to hear the word of God and respond to Him in an appropriate way. Unfortunately, many people are taught to be spiritually dependant on someone else. They are taught that they do not have direct access to deity. They believe that they are separate from God. God does not interfere with our beliefs or our actions. We have true freedom to act for ourselves and decide what to believe and how to act. When someone believes that they are separate from God, then they separate themselves from the source of wisdom and perfection that could otherwise be available to them. God is always present; it is we who are not paying attention. We need to wake up and join with God.

Sometimes in life we make mistakes which we regret, or develop habits which cause us problems and we find that we must make changes in how we handle ourselves in life. Change is always hard, but there are methods which help with the change and allow the healing process. Some mistakes have long term consequences and cause us pain and suffering for many years. It is important to be able to learn and grow from our mistakes and then move forward in life to minimize the agony we feel.

The first step in healing is to realize that the power to change is in the present. We cannot change the past; we can only work the miracle of healing in the present. Today is the day to put the past behind us and move forward. Today we should do everything in our power to make things right. If we have offended someone, then we should apologize and then be kinder and more loving towards them. If we have stolen something, we should return it. If we have damaged someone's property, we should get it fixed. For personal faults and defects we should make a conscious effort to improve our behavior. Unless we change ourselves, the situation will never improve. We can never change someone else. Our misery is there to tell us that we need to change something about ourselves. Now is the best time to initiate the change.

After we have made amends for our mistakes, we need to express regret about the wrong we committed. Admitting we were wrong, saying we are sorry, and truly expressing anguish allow us to be disassociated from those actions. When we are the only one affected then we only need to admit to ourselves that we made a mistake and feel regret over it. If we do not recognize our mistakes it is hard to ameliorate them.

Next we should ask for forgiveness for what we have done. If others are involved, we ask for their forgiveness. If we are the only one affected, we ask ourselves for forgiveness. If we feel that we have offended God, we ask God for forgiveness. Asking for and receiving a feeling of forgiveness from the ones we have offended goes a long way towards our healing and advancement towards peace and joy.

The last step in the healing process is probably the hardest. Let it go. It is often easier to forgive others than to forgive ourselves. We keep playing our mistakes over and over again in our minds. We become our mistakes instead of becoming our successes. When we make a mistake we do not have to accept the mistake. We do not need to let our mistakes dominate our lives or occupy our minds. Once we have learned the lessons of life and corrected our errors then we can move on and occupy our time and efforts in progressing in a positive way. Rehashing the past limits us to the past and does not allow us to create our future. Learn from the past, plan for the future, live in the present.

We all have experiences in this life which make us who we are. We are all one and our experience may help others around us more that it has helped us.

3. Testing

The third reason for being here on earth is to be tested, to find out who we really are and of what we are capable. The fetus in the womb has all her needs completely met by her mother. It is not until she is separated from her mother that she develops beyond her mother and finds herself eventually capable of caring for herself. She may even emulate her mother and have children of her own. We can grow and develop more when we work on our own problems, make our own decisions, and enjoy the consequences of our own decisions.

Many religions teach that this is a critical time of testing where God is sorting the good from the bad. The good go to Heaven and the bad go to Hell. Judgment in this life is very important to these people. They tend to judge everything through their opinion of good and evil. Either you are for God or against God. Either you are with Allah or the Great Satan. Unfortunately, no one is all good or all evil. Most of humanity is just trying to do their best to survive and fit in with others. People only desire the things that they believe will make them feel better, happier, and more joyful. The definition of good and evil depends greatly upon one's point of view. The heroes of the revolution are traitors when the revolution fails. George Washington would have been hung as traitor if Britain had won the Revolutionary

War. Today the enemies of the West are often heroes of the Middle East. In today's political arena the lines between good and evil are often blurred.

These judgments of right and wrong are always based on a person's core belief system. Often these beliefs are not even questioned. For example, in the western culture the most "blessed" people are viewed as white, wealthy, healthy, and Christian. The black, poor, infirm, and Non-Christian are considered cursed or out of God's favor. Eastern philosophy has the opposite belief system. It views the spiritual as brown (Indian/Asian), proudly poor, and cosmically mystic. People who are white (American), wealthy, and Christian are judged as materialistic and spiritually impoverished. It all really revolves around the idea that those who are similar to us are good and those who are different are bad. Such opinions of good and bad have no reality and passing judgments based on such opinions is best avoided.

Christ recommended that we not judge and criticize one another in the first place. He stated, "Don't criticize, and then you won't be criticized. For others will treat you as you treat them…" (Matthew 7:1-2)

When we are judging others we are really judging ourselves. Most of the imperfections of others which bother us do so because we are still struggling with the same or similar problems. Jesus taught further, "And why worry about a speck in the eye of a brother when you have a board in your own? Should you say, "Friend, let me help you get that speck out of your eye," when you can't even see because of the board in your own? Hypocrite! First get rid of the board. Then you can see to help your brother." (Matthew 7:3-5)

We clearly need to be more worried about our own development than about trying to correct those around us. We are to love our neighbor, not condemn them.

Some people see God as a condemning, judgmental God, like the God depicted in the Old Testament. The New Testament teaches us that God is a loving God who treats all mankind with love. He makes it to rain on the good and the bad. He gives us our freedom and allows us to live in the way we desire. We are free to create any kind of life or reality for ourselves that we desire. I believe that we are the ones that do all the judging, we judge ourselves, we judge others, we even judge and criticize God. It would be better for everyone if we would stop all the judging and become more like our Father in Heaven, experiencing unconditional love for ourselves and mankind.

The type of testing I see here for us in this earthly experience has more to do with our finding out for ourselves of what we are capable. Many of life's experiences provide opportunities to learn who we really are, what really matters to us, and who or what we truly love. We have the opportunity over and over again to redefine our lives and to make changes, to learn what works and what does not work. We are one with God and we have the ability to accomplish anything we desire, this earth life allows us to use our creative powers to make our life and change it in any way we want. Our personal choices teach us a lot about ourselves and our spiritual progression.

4. Fulfill Life's Mission

We participated in the planning of our lives before coming here to this earth. We agreed with others to interact with them and made commitments to them and to God. The place of our birth, our parents, and much about our opportunities in this life were determined long before our birth. We agreed to the conditions of our birth before coming to earth. We made choices prior to this earth life which affect our current condition, just like the choices we make in this life will affect our progression and condition in the lives to come. Often we are placed here on this earth in a specific place and time to accomplish a specific mission in life. For example, Jeremiah, a prophet in the Old Testament, was told that he was chosen to be the prophet before he was born. He came to earth at the time and circumstances that would allow him to accomplish his earthly mission as prophet to the Hebrew nation. (See Jeremiah 1:5)

Sometimes events of our lives do not make sense to us. We have difficulties that seem hard to overcome, or accept. People are born with handicaps and others develop illnesses which are life altering. Many times we are not able to see the purpose of such suffering.

I love fresh tree ripened peaches, and I plant peach trees almost everywhere I have lived. Whenever I prune my peach trees I feel sorry for the trees. I imagine that they have worked so hard to produce long green branches and have grown so tall. I almost apologize to them when I cut the branches shorter and remove many of the branches that have grown in the wrong places. Later, when I thin the fruit and remove at least half of the small hard green peaches it seems such a waste and it is difficult for me to do a thorough enough job. Even though it must seem devastating to the trees to lose so many branches and then have the precious ripening fruit stripped away and thrown in the garbage, I know that this is the best way to produce large, juicy peaches. If too many peaches are allowed to ripen on the tree, the fruit stays small, if fewer peaches are present they absorb more nutrition from the roots and grow much larger and desirable. The height of the tree has to be limited so that the ladders that I own can reach the peaches in the tops of the trees. The size and shape of the branches have to be trained and balanced with the strength of the roots. Everything I do for my trees is done to allow the trees to reach their full potential at producing the fruit I love.

I believe that God works with us in much the same manner. Sometimes we get more involved with producing more of the material things than spiritual things. We become prideful of our beautiful branches and forget that our destiny is to produce spiritual fruit. There are times in my life when I have undergone pruning by the hand of God. It often hurts badly and sometimes I do not understand the need to be pruned back. I have had my immature fruit thinned by the universe so that I had the strength in my roots to sustain the full ripening of the fruit that remained. When I encounter these types of difficult situations, I have to remember that God is the gardener and I am the fruit tree. He knows me and has more wisdom than I. He knows my destiny and purpose in this life better than I know it myself. I have to trust in Him to allow me to develop my goals and purpose in life to the fullest. When I am fully one with God I will see life from His perspective. I will fully understand the pruning process that I experienced.

The spinal injuries sustained by the actor Christopher Reeves (1952-2004) altered his life dramatically. Most would agree that he did his greatest work for mankind after his debilitating accident rather than before. Through his suffering and trials a legacy of hope and healing was left for others with similar problems with the creation of the Reeves-Irvine Research Center. I am inspired by his determination to live life to the fullest and to reach out to those around him. Many others have also dealt with seemingly disastrous experiences in an inspiring manner. It really is not important what occurs to us in our lives, but how we react and respond to the challenges of life.

We should remember that we were involved in the planning stages of this earth life and we agreed to the situations that we encounter here. It is an important part of our life to be close enough to God to be able to perceive our life's mission and to be able to follow the path to which we previously agreed. Often when we are on the path we find help and encouragement from the universe. Things will happen which seem to be coincidence, but are really coordinated by our actions and the laws operating in the universe. Unrelated activities come together at just the right time for our benefit. This phenomenon is known as synergism. For example, I recently purchased some land in the mountains of Arizona. I was working on building a storage shed there, but I ran low on lumber to finish the rafters. I had just stopped working to go twenty five miles into town to buy more lumber when the owners of the property next to mine came over to talk to me. They had a lot of lumber left over from a project which they had to take to the dump unless I was willing to take it. I was delighted. At the very moment I needed some wood, the universe provided me with an ample supply. I was able to finish my shed without a trip to town. God gives us exactly what we need at the moment we need it. The closer we are to our ideal the more the universe helps us on our way, the more we see synergism happening in our life.

CHAPTER III
WHERE AM I GOING?

1. Death

By training I am a scientist, a medical doctor by profession. I dedicated my life's work to the healing arts. It was in this framework that my search for my cosmic identity really began. I grew up with a Christian background, believing in an afterlife, so it always surprised me when a patient feared death so vigorously. To me, death was just a step in a new experience, some people take that step early in life, some take it later, but we all eventually take that step into the eternities. The reaction of some people to this next step in our progression was often filled with great fear, angst, and loss. I would be amazed that someone who truly believed in Christ and Eternal Life would act like they would never see their loved one again, or that they, in their own death would endure great pain and suffering. I observed as a physician, the pain and suffering seemed to occur prior to death, not after death. I have attended many deaths over the years, and the passing always brought peace to the deceased. No matter how much we cry out and are struggling in this life, death brings peace, relieves us of the pain and suffering of this world, and allows us to move on to the next experience.

If a person really believed in an afterlife with a loving God, then why would death be so traumatic? If a person feels so guilty about their actions that they are afraid to face a loving God, then maybe they should start changing their life now so they do not feel so guilty in the future. Perhaps today is the day to start trusting God more. If it is a close friend who is dying, then we might be saddened that we will not see them for a few years, until we too die and go to join with the dead.

It would be like when my older brother first went away to college. As children we were very close friends and I missed him a lot when he left home for the first time. I was left at home and in high school and I felt the loss keenly. It was hard at first, but I soon learned to make new friends and to make decisions for myself. I had to grow up a bit and mature, but it was a good experience for both of us. If we are the ones about to die, then it should give us comfort that we will soon see all of our friends and relatives that have gone on before us. When I finally went to college, I visited my brother from time to time on campus, and even now in mid life we see each other once in a while. My own children have grown up and left home and I see them occasionally. I know that they are okay and they are happy with where they are. I believe that when people die, they are also okay and are happy with where they are.

I do not wish to trivialize the loneliness and grief that some people feel when a very close loved one dies, especially when the loss is sudden, premature, or unexpected. I wish to reassure everyone that their loved ones are safe and happy. Someday soon a reunion with them will occur which will bring joy and healing. Often the dead we mourn are very aware of our loss and are trying to comfort us in the way that they are able. If we can be open and sensitive to our feelings and intuition, we may be able to feel their presence.

2. Spirit World

Many books have been written about the spirit world and the activities there. Everything that I have read that talks about a person's personal experience with the afterlife indicates that this is a place of peace, joy, and healing. There the love of God is ever present and people regain their connection with the universal energy in an obvious manner. After our death, our spirits go to this place of light and joy where we begin to remember our true selves. We remember, and review, everything we have thought, said, or done. This period of life review is part of the healing process where we learn from our life's experiences and find understanding about our life's path and our true destiny. We are able to review and learn from our mistakes, as well as our successes. We realize how we affected others who crossed our path in life and how they affected us. We find the answers to our questions, heal relationships with others, and find joy and happiness in the process.

The spirit world is a place of constant activity and learning. It contains libraries of information, schools for our spiritual education, and workshops to help us master important skills. Everything is done in a spirit of joy and according to our true desire to progress and develop spiritually. It is a busy place of preparation and education in a perfect, enjoyable atmosphere.

Part of the work done in the spirit world is performed to benefit us here on earth. Spirit guides are there to actively help us on our life's journey. They constantly pay attention to us and our difficulties and are there to give us guidance and inspiration. They help arrange the events in this earth life which contribute to our personal growth and experience. They are the "Guardian Angels", the "Sentinel Angels", and the "Warrior Angels" that people often call upon for help and protection. Many of these beings have lived on this earth already and have a vivid awareness of the difficulties we incur during our earth life. Some of these spirits are beings that have never been to this earthly realm, but have developed spiritual skills essential in performing their tasks. There are councils who meet together and discuss our decisions, activities, and difficulties and then work together to meet our needs and help us fulfill our life's work.

There is much to be done in the world of spirits. Those there are engaged in healing others and being healed, teaching and being taught, guiding and being guided, counseling and being counseled. They are creating, planning, and joyfully living with all of humanity. This is a realm of infinite joy and infinite possibilities. It is a place where we are able to remember and realize our true selves. Jesus described the spirit world perfectly when He spoke of it to the thief hanging on the cross next to His. "And Jesus (said), "Today you will be with me in Paradise. This is a solemn promise."" (Luke 23:43)

3. Ultimate Destiny

The spirit world is where we prepare for our next experience. We are eternal beings and our existence does not persist forever in the spirit world. There we are preparing further for our next life. Some people believe that the next life is here on earth again, that we are trapped in a never ending cycle of rebirth. Others believe that we incarnate on other planets in other galaxies or dimensions. I believe that we prepare for the resurrection and our life as immortal glorious beings.

There is not much written about our life after the resurrection. We are given more about the now than about the future. This is to help us be focused on this life, this incarnation, and this experience. We are not to be living too much in the past or too much in the future. We ought to remember the past, plan for the future, but live in the present. Everything about spiritual development emphasizes the importance of the present and taking care of the task at hand. We should be enjoying our present condition and not just dreaming for a better afterlife. We will probably be at least as happy there as we are here. Our minds are the same here as there. Death does nothing to alter our basic nature. If we are not happy now, then we need to change things in our current life until we are happy. We are not meant to suffer in this life to be blessed with happiness in the next life. We are intended to experience joy and happiness now and everyday. If we are not happy, then we are somehow distant from our true selves and we are separated from the universal source of joy, God's spirit. The only thing we ever lack is a closeness with God's spirit. When we feel that we need something in our life to be fulfilled, we are really feeling a yearning for a return to God's presence. Material things, worldly relationships, or life's accomplishments will never fill that void. The only resolution of that feeling is to grow spiritually.

I have heard many people say that we are either destined for heaven or hell. Like we are weighed on a big balance and if we were good enough we go to heaven and otherwise we go to hell. I have even heard people say that someone is going to hell because they have not accepted Christ as their Savior. First I would say that it is not up to us to be judging our neighbors. We are to be involved with loving them. I cannot judge anyone else; I do not know their circumstances and their secret thoughts. We have received very direct instructions from Christ about not judging others. Secondly, I believe that every one of us will receive the opportunity to accept Christ sometime, if not in this life, then in the next life. Thirdly, life is not as black and white as this implies. No one is all good. No one is all bad. Everyone's circumstances and opportunities are different.

Just because someone was baptized it does not make them spiritually advanced. Just because someone is devoutly religious in a different faith than ours it does not make them evil. God will judge each of us according to our spiritual understanding and the intentions of our actions. It may well be better for someone who has never even heard of Christ than for a Christian who ignores his baptismal covenants. Finally, I believe that God is more loving and more capable than that. God is not a failure and I think that God created us to succeed, not to fail. I think the power of God can make up for any deficiencies that we have personally. I think that most, if not all, of God's children will live throughout the eternities in peace and happiness. We will essentially all be in a better place in the hereafter than we are here on this earth.

After the resurrection, we are intended to eventually become divine, like God, like Christ. The mission and life of Christ was to illustrate to the whole world the path we are to follow. We are born in to this world as mortal beings, we die, and our bodies are separated from our spirits. In the resurrection we are reborn as glorious, perfected, immortal, godlike beings. Christ's life is a direct example of our lives. Christ is God's Son, we are God's children. Christ was born human, we are born human. Christ died, we will all die. Christ's body was laid in the tomb; our bodies will be cremated, buried, mummified, and laid to rest. Christ's spirit went to the spirit world; our spirits will go to the spirit world. Christ resurrected, his body and spirit were reunited, we will resurrect, and our body and spirit will reunite. Christ went to God and became exalted, glorified, and godlike; we will return to God and become exalted, glorified, and godlike.

Many people are uncomfortable with idea that humans will eventually become god-like. They think that this idea is somehow offensive to the idea of One God. They do not realize that we are all one and we are one with God. They forget that this earth life is an illusion and we are already much more capable than is readily apparent.

There is only one God because God encompasses everything and every individual. One Jehovah, One Allah, One Elohim, One Krishna are all one God. When the concept of one God was first realized by organized religion people took the idea of oneness and corrupted it to their separate thinking. Instead of allowing the concept of multiple enlightened beings linked together as one to continue they changed the ancient documents from the plural to the singular. (Ezra, the scribe in the Book of Ezra of the Old Testament changed the creation story in Genesis) They take the three gods of Christianity and unite them into one God and call it a mystery. They feel that only uninspired pagans would believe in multiple gods. Even Christ was accused of being blasphemous when He stated the truth about His relationship to the Father.

The concept of God and oneness is very difficult for us to perceive in this three dimensional reality. Also, the idea of God has multiple meanings. It can mean an advanced, enlightened being with glory, immortality, and astonishing power, or it can mean a specific entity that encompasses everything. It is certainly reasonable to realize that there may be more than one glorious, advanced being and yet there is only one God.

As an analogy, there are many waves in the ocean, but there is only one ocean. Furthermore, I know of many fathers, but my father is Jay Robertson, and the fact I have grown to become a father myself does not diminish Jay in any way. It actually makes my father proud of me when I become a father myself, he becomes greater, a grandfather. I can easily worship God as the creator, founder, and Father of the entire universe, and Jesus Christ as my personal Savior, and still realize that there may be an infinite number of universes, dimensions, and advanced beings. When I develop to the point of becoming godlike, I join fully with God, and it only brings joy both to me, and to my God, whom I honor with my oneness.

The goal is to be in reality one with God. This is accomplished through love. Love for God, love for others, and love for ourselves. The Holy Spirit works in each one of us to that end. I know that I currently am more capable and have greater potential than meets the eye. It is my task to develop this potential into godlike abilities. It does not diminish God in any way to believe that humans are progressing towards godliness. It just increases my awe and respect for God and Christ to know how far I have to progress to reach that level. I have the capacity to walk on water; it is just my lack of spiritual development that prevents me from doing so.

The parable of the prodigal son relates to us in this earthly sojourn. "A man had two sons. When the younger told his father, "I want my share of your estate now, instead of waiting until you die!" his father agreed to divide his wealth between his sons.

A few days later this younger son packed all his belongings and took a trip to a distant land, and there wasted all his money on parties and prostitutes.

About the time his money was gone a great famine swept over the land, and he began to starve. He persuaded a local farmer to hire him to feed his pigs. The boy became so hungry that even the pods he was feeding the swine looked good to him. And no one gave him anything.

When he finally came to his senses, he said to himself, "At home even the hired men have food enough and to spare, and here I am, dying of hunger! I will go home to my father and say, "Father, I have sinned against both heaven and you, and am no longer worthy of being called your son. Please take me on as a hired man.""

So he returned home to his father. And while he was still a long distance away, his father saw him coming, and was filled with loving pity and ran and embraced him and kissed him.

His son said to him, "Father, I have sinned against heaven and you, and am not worthy of being called your son—"

But his father said to the slaves, "Quick! Bring the finest robe in the house and put it on him. And a jeweled ring for his finger; and shoes! And kill the calf we have in the fattening pen. We must celebrate with a feast, for this son of mine was dead and has returned to life. He was lost and is found." So the party began." (Luke 15:11-24)

We were with God prior to deciding to leave Him to live in this realm, like the son leaving his father to go to a far away land. We spend our time searching after the pleasures of this world, thinking that they will make us happy. Left to our own devices, we will always end up miserable, because we are separated from God. Until we come to our senses and return home to our Father we will never be truly happy. Many of us are afraid of returning home to God because of our guilt over our earthly behavior and our desire to separate ourselves from God in the first place. We think that God will judge us and find us unworthy. We have the attitude of "I am not worthy of being called your son (or daughter)." In reality, God is anxious to have us return home to join with Him again. He is all loving. The party and celebration begins when we return to God. We are the ones who separate ourselves from God. When we remove our resistance to Him, then the Holy Spirit can enter our life, provide healing, and reunite us with God. We really are all one and we are one with God.

Many theologians agree with mankind's divine destiny. Deification is part of the theology of many Christian religions. In the second century Saint Irenaeus, one of the most important Christian writers of his time, wrote of man's eternal destiny, "If the Word became a man, it was so men may become gods." (Irenaeus, *Against Heresies,* bk. 5, pref.) He also wrote, "Do we cast blame on him [God] because we were not made gods from the beginning, but were at first created merely as men, and then later as gods? Although God has adopted this course out of his pure benevolence, that no one may charge him with discrimination or stinginess, he declares, *"I* have said, Ye are gods; and all of you are sons of the Most High.'" (Irenaeus, *Against Heresies,* 4.38)

Saint Clement of Alexandria wrote, *"Yea,* I say, the Word of God became a man so that you might learn from a man how to become a god" (Clement of Alexandria, *Exhortation to the Greeks, 1)*

We are God's children. Our true heritage and destiny is to develop into glorious, creative, joyful beings and to participate in the work of creation and godhood for all eternity.

CHAPTER IV
ETERNAL TRUTH

1. God Exists

There are basic eternal truths which exist and which are in operation now and throughout our earthly experience. They may be difficult to prove, but their existence can be demonstrated through personal experience. These truths do not depend on our belief for their existence, they affect all of us whether we are aware of them or not. We can all benefit by learning them, but just having knowledge is not very useful without the wisdom to understand how to use the insight. For example, the law of gravity is important to comprehend in our current existence. In our world it is useful to know that things fall when dropped. If you are about to step off a high cliff, it is useful to be prepared. Independent of your knowledge of this law, you will fall if you step over the edge of a cliff. Ignorance of natural laws does not prevent a person from experiencing the effects of those truths.

God exists. This is the most basic truth. There is some greater power or being we call God. We may use a variety of names for God such as the Universal Force, the Source Energy, the First Cause, Elohim, Jehovah, Krishna, or Allah, but we are still talking about the same entity. The nature of God has been argued about for many centuries and there is certainly no consensus on the nature of God today. It is impossible to prove to someone else that God exists. All the clever arguments of the philosophers avail nothing in this arena. God may reveal Himself to an individual and that becomes a personal knowledge of God, but it is not proof to another person of God's existence. The only proof that there is a God is that sense within oneself, that feeling of truth that one has in his consciousness that knows that God exists. Only God can reveal His existence to a person.

If someone were to prove a scientific theory he would use the scientific method, showing through reproducible experimentation that the facts support the hypothesis. The same is true with spirituality; the proof of God can only be obtained through spiritual experimentation and experience. One would not use philosophy to prove that a new medication works to prevent heart attacks. We cannot use words to prove spiritual truth. Spirit is felt, it is intuitive, it is an internal sensation which a person has to obtain for himself. The spirit of truth works in all people who will listen. God is eternal and never ending. He has always existed and will always exist. He does not need us to believe in Him. He does not need anything from us. He is perfect in and of Himself. He is Allah, Elohim, The Father. He knows everything and understands everything.

The nature of God has been discussed and argued about for all of human history. Western philosophers and theologians differed greatly on their description of God. The ancients anthropomorphized God and made Him into a being with human emotions such as love, anger, and jealousy. Later Aristotle described God as a perfect universal force. The early Christians accepted this idea of Godhood and applied it to the Trinity believing in a God without body, parts, or passions. It became common for people to believe that God could only be a disembodied force in the universe. Thinking that He is a physical being would somehow deny His perfection and magnificence. Many people believe that "God is Spirit" and ignore the fact that just because spirit is one aspect of God, there may be many more descriptors of God which could and have been used. God is love, God is wise, God is perfect, God is omniscience, omnipotent, omnipresent, omniloving. He will never be harmed. He needs nothing to be complete. Just as we are complex beings made up of lots of qualities and materials, God is complex also. He is so complex that people have argued about the nature of God for all of human history.

When I was young I read a book that taught the idea that the Bible describes the interactions of primitive man with a more advanced alien civilization. It suggested that the human race was created by these beings through genetic engineering with the primates of the day. We were a science experiment for them, and as such they continued to show interest in our progress. They came down from time to time to teach and help our civilization (their experiment) to progress. This viewpoint made a lot of sense to me. It explained in my mind how Adam could walk with God, how Jacob could wrestle with an angel, how Moses could talk to God face to face, how Mohammed could be taught by an angel. It suggested that Jesus was born of Mary who was impregnated by an alien, and so Christ was half human and half alien. He supposedly met his alien father when he sojourned in the wilderness for forty days and was taught many advanced methods which allowed him to perform the miracles during his life. This book stated that these alien beings are still watching us and sometimes visit us, which explains the UFO sightings and rumors of alien abductions. I used to love to read many science fiction types of books. Advanced civilizations and alien cultures were well within my realm of understanding. I sometimes think that this idea is closer to the truth than what some religions teach about God, angels, and humans.

People are willing to kill and persecute others for not agreeing with their perception of God. We would probably all be better off if we would admit to ourselves and others that there is much about God that we do not know or understand. It is only what God has revealed about Himself to humanity that is knowable. The rest is just man's imagination and personal philosophy. The only thing on which we can all truly depend is that God does exist. He is alive and well, is still very interested in humanity, and knows us personally.

2. Law of Attraction

One of the greatest and most powerful universal laws is the Law of Attraction. This law is simply stated, "like attracts like". We see this law in operation everyday of our lives and we can use this law to attract anything we desire into our lives.

People tend to group together with other people similar to themselves. In High School we congregated into distinct groups. There were the smart people, the cheerleaders, the jocks, the druggies, the skaters, the punks, etc. As teenagers try to find their own identity they may cross the social lines, but in general they feel most comfortable with those who are similar to themselves. Throughout our lives we experience the same tendency. We socialize with people in our own socioeconomic class. We tend to segregate ourselves from others' cultures, religious beliefs, professions, etc. We cling together according to our behavior and actions, even the way we dress and talk. We enter into relationships with others who we attract into our lives. This is all due to the universal law of attraction. The only reason why we may be involved with someone much different from ourselves is that we have similar lessons in life that need to be learned, or there may be similar goals that cause the attraction. Opposites do not attract. Oil and water do not mix. The wealthy are not attracted to the poor, and the poor do not feel comfortable with the wealthy. The educated do not socialize with the uninformed.

A group of people make up the feel of the local environment. Their attitudes and beliefs create the quality of the region in which they live. When a person moves to a new location it is often done unconsciously because they relate personally with the other people in the area. Individuals feel more comfortable when they live in an area with the weather and demographics with which they are compatible. This is one reason why urban renewal programs are so difficult. It is almost impossible to change the belief system of those in the neighborhood no matter how much money is spent. The same problem occurs in foreign countries. It is difficult to impose a democracy or a western lifestyle from the outside. Progress will always be met with resistance until the core beliefs of the citizens have been altered. Education is still the best way to improve society. It is certainly fine for people to live in whatever way they desire. The problems occur when others try to impose a lifestyle against their will.

Most people do not realize that the law of attraction goes much deeper than just our actions; it also works with our thoughts and attitudes. What we think about all day long will be attracted into our lives. The thoughts we have become attitudes and the attitudes become behaviors. The behaviors become habits, and the habits create who we are. It all starts with our thoughts.

For example, if a person has basically a cheerful, upbeat, optimistic outlook on life he will act in a friendly, outgoing manner. He will smile and be cheerful when interacting with others around him. His attitude will affect the feelings of those around him, contributing to the overall levity of that setting. Those around him that share in his optimism and cheerfulness will gravitate towards him and as time goes on, a friendly group will develop. On the other hand, if a person has the opposite outlook on life, he will only see the bad in a situation, and often he will be down and depressed. He will act in a more negative manner. His sadness or anger will also be felt in a group and people will often shy away from his moodiness. A group of similar minded people will congregate around him, forming a clique of backbiters and gossipers. Instead of a happy supportive group, a group of angry, irritable, and depressed people will form.

In my office there was a group of about three employees who hung out together. They always took breaks together and even socialized after work hours. I often had complaints about them from others in the office. They seemed often to be the ones who instigated conflict in the office and said and did put downs to other employees. Eventually they were terminated and had to find other jobs. I also remember another small group of employees who gathered together and socialized. They seemed more upbeat and often talked of ways to improve the office and help other employees. They would come to me with suggestions for improvement and reminded me to celebrate employee birthdays and individual accomplishments. They stayed on for many years and became valuable assets to the office. The attitudes and behaviors of both groups lead to very different outcomes.

The universe also directly responds to our thoughts and actions. What we put out into the universe will come back to us. Our thoughts are real and influence the world around us. Thoughts generate electrical signals in our nervous systems and those signals create an electromagnetic field which can be physically measured. This is what physicians measure when they do an EEG or perform a sleep study.

This is the basis for the lie detector. This electrical field spreads outward from our bodies and interacts with other similar fields in our vicinity. Other fields also spread outward from their individual sources and mix and blend creating the fabric of our universe. Our individual thoughts resonate with other thoughts and spiritual forces in the universe returning to us events and opportunities based on those thoughts. Our thoughts attract into our lives the experiences and objects that resonate with them. The emotion we have behind the thought gives it power. The greater the feelings behind a thought, the greater the force generated. The universe responds directly to the force and nature of our thoughts.

If we are fearful, then we will be given situations that reinforce our fear. If we are confident, we will often succeed at our tasks. Our thoughts directly influence the world around us. Like ripples on a pond they spread out into the universe and return to us and bring us what we have truly wanted. We directly create the conditions of our life by our daily thoughts. If we are not happy with our current situation in life then we need to pay more attention to our thoughts and change the ones that do not lead to our desires. We have emotions to allow us to know if we are thinking properly according to our true desires. If we feel depressed, angry, or powerless then we need to change what we think about until we feel joyful, happy, and excited. Most of the misery and suffering we endure in this life we actually create ourselves because we have not mastered this one basic law.

The universe does not judge our thoughts. It gives us exactly what we think about. For example, if we have an old car that is worn out and needs replacing we probably would desire a new car. If we think about a new car, look at new car magazines, shop for new cars, dream about how nice it would feel to drive around in our new car, believe that we will soon get a new car, then we will soon get a new car. We can be happy inside knowing that we will soon get a new car. By holding the emotion of excited anticipation, like a child on Christmas Eve, we tell the universe that we are ready to receive our new car. Feeling that way can only make us happy, even while still driving our old car. If we think about how rotten our old car is, how much we hate our old car, how unreliable our old car is, how embarrassed we are about driving our old car, then the universe will keep us in our old, unreliable, embarrassing car. What we think about is what we get. Even if we are thinking we do not want something, we will receive it because that is what we are thinking about. It is what we are paying attention to that we receive.

We get to choose our thoughts every second of the day. No one can tell us what to think. No one can force us to think a certain way. We choose what to think about. Our emotions tell us if what we are thinking about is really what we want or if we are wasting our mental creative ability on negative thoughts. If the thoughts make us feel happy then we are on the right path. If our thoughts make us feel miserable, then we are thinking wrongly. We choose to be happy or sad by the way we think. The universe will give us what we are thinking about, either reinforcing our sad or happy emotions.

Recently, my son was driving home from a trip to California. He was nervous to be driving alone because he lacked experience in traveling by himself. Throughout the trip he kept on thinking that he did not want to get into an accident. He worried about accidents and could not get the idea of an accident out of his mind. Sure enough, as he approached Phoenix, his rear tire blew out for no apparent reason; he spun around several times at 75 mph before crashing into a car next to him. He sustained minor injuries and substantial damage to his car. The universe gave him the exact experience about which he was thinking. During travel it would be better to enjoy the scenery, to imagine traveling down the road safely, and to be confident in your ability to complete the trip. These more joyful thoughts would allow a more joyful experience.

Everyone wants things in life, and we can obtain anything we desire. If we want to be healthy, we can concentrate on health and the proper function of our bodies. If we want more money we can think about having plenty of money instead of worrying so much about not having enough. We can pay our bills cheerfully and be thankful for having enough to pay the ones we can. We can be generous with the poor because we know that we have plenty of money. We should never feel like we are being selfish for wanting things. The universe is infinite and there is enough for everyone. We do not worry about having more health than another or of depriving someone else of health just because we are so healthy. We do not need to worry about depriving someone else of something just because we want it. There is plenty for everyone to have their desires answered by the universe. Much of the poverty and lack in society is caused by the way impoverished people think and view the world and their place in it. They are often so busy focusing on their lack that they do not realize that they are actually reinforcing their poverty. It is important to focus on what we desire, not the lack of what we desire. Our emotions are the best guide we have to proper thinking. If our thoughts bring us joy then we are thinking the right kinds of thoughts and we can obtain joyful fulfilling lives. It is also very important to be thankful for what we have. Why would the universe give us more of something if we do not appreciate what we have already received? Our attitude of gratitude allows the universe to bless us with abundance.

When I was in college planning to apply to medical school, my career advisor told me that I had very little chance of being accepted to the medical school of my choice. My grades were not that wonderful and better applicants had been turned down by that particular medical college before. I really wanted to attend that school, and I felt very strongly that everything would work out for me. Rather than be discouraged, I kept a very positive image of my attending medical school in my mind. Later in the year I took the medical college entrance exam (MCAT) and I scored very well on that test. I applied to several medical schools and was accepted to my first choice of colleges. I am sure that having an optimistic outlook helped me throughout the application process. My mental projection allowed me to score well on the entrance exam and to overcome the barriers before me.

3. Law of the Harvest

The Tsunami on December 26, 2004 in the Indian Ocean which killed over 150,000 people was caused by mankind. It was not an act of retribution from a vengeful God who wanted to punish humans. God would never cause such misery and destruction. He loves us as He loves Himself. Our suffering is His suffering. He hurts when we hurt. We are one, we are all connected. In the Book of Enoch, Enoch is amazed that God weeps for the suffering of the human race. Our sorrows are His sorrows, our joy is His joy.

The Tsunami was caused by humans not being aware of the consequences of their thoughts and creative power, including their violent behavior and negativity. Everything around us is alive. The atoms and molecules of inanimate objects are full of activity and energy. The earth is alive and filled with living things. The spirit of God permeates all things and fills the world with His wisdom. God's spirit is the same type of energy that we radiate with our thoughts. Our thoughts generate the same type of spiritual power as God does. We participate in the creation of our reality and the events that happen here. We are one with each other and we are one with God. All of us are linked by an energy field. Everything we think and all of our actions put out energy into the world and into the universe. When a large number of people in the world are pursuing negative actions of violence and war, a large amount of negative energy is created on earth and this affects the world. When even more people watch these violent actions on the TV and media sources and argue among themselves about the validity of the war or become angry and have hostile thoughts and actions towards others, a great amount of negative energy is produced and sent out into the world. The world has seen a great increase in the amount of violence, terrorism, and war in recent years. The attacks of September 11, 2001, the anthrax, the attack of Iraq, the killing of innocent minorities both in the US and Middle East have all been graphically displayed for the world to watch on TV, cable, and the internet. The earth, as a living organism, responds to this huge amount of negativity in its own natural way. Earthquakes, volcanoes, and storms are some of the methods by which the earth releases its negative energy.

Most people are ignorant of the way their thoughts affect the earth itself. Our thoughts affect each other. Our thoughts affect our environment. We all have heard of someone with a "green thumb". The garden responds to that person's love of nature and their positive thoughts. Our thoughts are very powerful and have the energy and power to create all things. They have the power to cause harm and destruction also. The earth responds to our collective thoughts by giving us back what we send out. There are many people who do understand this relationship and put out positive, healing energy directed to the environment in their daily meditations and prayers. We need more people who respond to the violence of others by positive means, healing, love, and compassion, instead of by negative means, hate, strife, and violence.

We are like small children who have found a box of matches. We sneak up to our rooms and close the door so that we are all alone. We know that the matches are forbidden by our parents and they would be angry with us if they found out we had the matches. We do not really care what our parents tell us because we just pick the rules we want to follow anyway, which rules we think we can ignore and get away with without being caught. What could happen just by lighting a few of them? We strike a match and watch it burn, the flame is so pretty and fascinating. We blow it out and drop it in the wastebasket. We light another and watch it burn, and another, and another. Suddenly, we notice the wastebasket we were using, which was full of paper, is flaming up on fire. We panic. We do not know what to do. We are afraid. So we quickly, quietly leave the room and close the door behind us. We run out of the house, afraid of getting in trouble and being punished by our parents. We end up going to a friend's house to play, but very soon our play is interrupted by the sound of fire engines. Our house is burning and that causes a great loss and destruction in our family. Maybe someone in our family even died, not being able to get out of the burning house on time.

We do not fully realize that the violent behavior and thoughts in our society have a direct effect on the environment to which the earth responds. In the fire analogy, we were not being punished by God for playing with matches. Things burn and playing with matches is dangerous. Most of us realize this with matches and fires. Thoughts are dangerous too, and the way we think about others and treat them can cause consequences that are far reaching. If we really understood how important and powerful our thoughts can be, we would be much more careful about what we thought about all day long and how we use our minds. Thoughts are the most basic and important creations of our minds. Thoughts are real and have infinite potential. A bolt of lightning and the small current in a hand held flashlight are both phenomena of electricity. Individual thoughts may be weak but collective thought can create a great amount of power. They may produce even enough power to move mountains and cause earthquakes. The collective consciousness may even create universes.

In the Book of Deuteronomy of the Old Testament, Moses teaches the people of Israel that if they disobey the Judaic law, famine and drought will occur. The earth would not respond to their efforts to survive. If they were obedient, the earth would bring forth a fullness of the harvest and they would have plenty to eat. These truths and many others like them have often been misunderstood by mankind. We are taught by our churches that God rewards the righteous and punishes the sinner. That He is an angry and a vengeful God. Nothing could be further than the truth. He loves us, we are one with Him, when we suffer, He suffers, when we are joyful, He has joy. Moses was trying to teach the laws of attraction to the people. What we do affects the earth. What we think affects our circumstances. Not because God will respond, but because the environment responds to us. If we want peace and happiness, we have to be peaceful and happy inside.

It is critically important that we change the way we think and react to the negativity in the world around us. The recent hurricane that destroyed New Orleans and neighboring regions (2005) demonstrates the urgency of the situation. More disasters are likely to follow. The world is raging out of control all around us threatening to kill people and to destroy many of our cities and towns. These natural disasters, added to the man made destruction in the world, strain our resources and our ability to maintain the global economy. Interruption of food production and distribution will certainly follow.

Widespread suffering and loss is very likely. We need to act now. We can no longer afford to postpone the extreme need to join together in peace and work together to heal the earth and our selves.

One of the most important laws of the universe is known as the law of the harvest. This is stated as "you reap what you sow". This law is well known and has been written about in numerous books. It is present in almost all religions. The New Testament conveys this principle in Galatians. The apostle Paul wrote, "Don't be misled; remember that you can't ignore God and get away with it: a man will always reap just the kind of crop he sows! If he sows to please his own wrong desires, he will be planting seeds of evil and he will surely reap a harvest of spiritual decay and death; but if he plants the good things of the Spirit, he will reap the everlasting life which the Holy Spirit gives him. And let us not get tired of doing what is right, for after a while we will reap a harvest of blessing if we don't get discouraged and give up. That's why whenever we can we should always be kind to everyone, and especially to our Christian brothers." (Galatians 6:7-10)

Paul is very clear about this law and this law is very simple, "What a man sows that shall he reap." Almost as simple as the law of gravity, "What goes up must come down." What ever we do in this life will come back and affect us in some way. If we have hurt others, we will get hurt by others. If we forgive others we will be forgiven. If we are kind others will be kind to us. What happens to us in our lives is a very good indication of how we are treating others and what kinds of thoughts we encourage. Paul encourages us to do good deeds to all men because we are really doing good deeds to ourselves. We are all one.

The resistance we have to view all of mankind as our self is shown by Paul's qualifier, "especially to our Christian brothers". It is interesting that Paul, even though he lived close to the time of Christ, still did not completely view his neighbor as himself, especially if they were not of the same faith. We are still of the same mind set. We are much more likely to show kindness to someone with whom we identify. Like begets like. If we are helpful, we will receive help.

In eastern philosophies the Law of the Harvest is known as the law of Karma, our choices will come back to us in this life or another. Today people often say, "What goes around comes around". The way we treat others is the way we are treated. If we desire to have good things happen to us in our lives, we need to be doing good for those around us. We interact with others every day, our spouses, our children, our parents, our friends, our co-workers, our neighbors, and even those we dislike or with whom we disagree. It is best to treat every one around us as we would like to be treated. If there is an argument, be quick to forgive and give the other the benefit of the doubt in the matter. Many times we get so caught up in being right that we lose sight of what is truly important. We assume that we gain more by winning the conflict, but often contention causes everyone to lose in the long run.

From the law of the harvest we understand that if we treat someone poorly, in an angry, argumentative way then we will in turn be treated by others in a contentious way. We are directly responsible for our choices and our thoughts and we will personally bear the consequences of our choices, whether for good or ill. If we are quick to make peace, others will make peace with us. If we take something from others, we will have things taken from us. It really is not God punishing us or rewarding us, it is the natural, universal law of the harvest in action, just like God is not punishing us if we ignore the law of gravity and walk off a cliff.

There really is not a right way or a wrong way; there are behaviors and attitudes that work and those that do not work, depending on what your goals are. If your goal is to be filled with anger, frustration, and conflict, then treat others harshly, but if you desire peace and tranquility then love others and treat them as yourself. There are consequences to our thoughts, our actions, and our choices with which God does not interfere. He tries to teach us about the universal laws and principles, but He leaves it up to us to listen and learn. Life is a great teacher, and most of us eventually learn, some people only seem to learn through pain and sorrow. It is like the child who has to be burnt before he learns not to play with fire.

4. Law of One

We are all connected to one another and to God. We are spiritually connected by our eternal kinship with each other. We are physically connected through the electrical vibrations of our body and spirit. It is an illusion of this life that we are separate entities. When we look around and see ourselves distinct and separated from others we are deceived. Anyone who teaches that one group is better than another is creating conflict. When religions teach that one group will be saved and not another they are in error. Anyone who teaches exclusion is giving a false perspective. We are all God's children. He loves us all unconditionally. He allows all of us to learn and grow at our own pace. What happens to one of us affects all of us. There would be substantially less violence and conflict in the world if everyone understood this universal law. "Do unto others as you would have others do unto you" really becomes "treat yourself well". When we realize that we are those others out there in the world then we would naturally want to treat them well because we are them and they are us.

Sometimes I look around and see myself as others. I see the store clerk and think, "There I am being a clerk." I see a wealthy person and think, "There I am being wealthy and driving my fancy car." I see a beggar and think, "There I am begging for my sustenance." It really changes my perspective when I realize that I am all those people and infinitely more. Recently, my wife and I were having a mild confrontation about ice cream flavors. I realized how silly this all was and I stopped and thought to myself, "Here I am arguing with myself about nothing." I shut my mouth and ended the contention.

Many people have problems seeing past the illusion of being separated from each other. I am reminded of the dual nature of light. In some instances light acts individually like little particles of light called photons. Under other circumstances it behaves more like an energy wave, or electromagnetic radiation. We are beings of light connected through our collective energy wave, even though we seem to be individuals on this earth. When light streams down on us from the sun we do not see individual particles, we see a collective field of energy, pouring down over the whole earth. The electrical signal that your body generates radiates outward from you infinitely. It has no end. It mixes with the electrical signals from others and is affected by those signals. It affects them also. It is impossible for your signal to be separated from all the others. They all blend together and make the collective consciousness.

We are one with God also. God's spirit or field permeates the universe just as our field or spirit permeates the universe. We are joined together electrically and spiritually and cannot be separated from God. The fact that we are one with God means that we are infinitely capable to carry out any activity we desire.

We are like a person who has a million dollar bank account but only thinks he has one hundred dollars. He may want to purchase something he really needs or desires, but does not because he believes he cannot afford it. He will never spend more than one hundred dollars. Even if someone told him he had lots of money in the bank he would not believe them until he knew from whence the money had come. We are spiritual millionaires, sharing a spiritual bank account with God. We are blinded to this reality by the illusion of this world. We have unlimited potential, but we think we are limited. We are eternal, but we think we are ephemeral. Christ showed us the kinds of things we could accomplish if we just had a little faith. We are one with God, we can accomplish anything.

Most of us limit our abilities due to doubt and fear. Doubt and fear limit people more than any other emotion. They prevent us from obtaining what we desire and from fulfilling our potential. Doubt and faith cannot exist together. Either we believe that we can do something or we have doubt about our ability. Either we have faith that God will help us or we doubt God's ability. Fear is not the same as caution. Fear is an emotion which prevents us from action. It blocks progression, stifles faith. Caution makes us think, plan, and be watchful before moving forward. Caution is what makes us look both ways before crossing the street. Fear prevents us from stepping off the curb. It is fine to be cautious and consider carefully when making plans for our future, but once we have decided on our course of action we need to be full of faith and confidence. Let doubt and fear go and focus more on love and joyful living. We seem to have a great ability to visualize failure rather than success. Five minutes of joyfully visualizing the life we desire on a daily basis will do much for our ability to manifest it. We are often discouraged from daydreaming, yet we would be better off if we daydreamed more and worried less.

I am often amazed by how much we doubt ourselves. I often talk to others about my beliefs, especially the idea that we influence our lives by our thoughts and people tell me that they cannot do it. I tell them of my personal experiences and they say that they are not as smart as I am, or they are not as capable. It is the self doubt that prevents them. This demonstrates exactly what I was trying to tell them in the first place. Their self doubt holds them in their current condition. These people do not realize that they are creating their life through their thinking even while they are denying to me that they can. The universe rewards us all equally. We all are creating our lives with every thought. We all have the capability to focus and direct our thoughts towards that which we desire; it is up to us to develop it.

Christ taught, "…When you did it to these my brothers you were doing it to me!" (Matthew 25:40) We are all one. We have the potential to be like Christ and help others like Christ did. We often think we do not have the time, or talent, or ability to help others when in fact we have God like abilities. We are one with God.

5. The Law of Now

Time is an illusion. The only time that exists is now. We move from one now to the next now. Now is all we really have. Now is when we think. Now is when we act. Now is when we pray. Now is when we work. We need to be aware of how we feel now.

Many of us spend all of our time and energy reminiscing about the past. We wax nostalgic about the good old days and we truly believe that the best time has past us by and now is not as pleasant as the past. The memory we have of the past is often deceitful. We forget the struggles and difficulties that we endured and only entertain nostalgic memories. Often the people that are prone to this thinking were no happier when the past was now than they are now. They complained and grumbled about the 60's when it was now but thought the 50's were wonderful. When the 80's came they were terrible but the 60's and 70's were great.

Some of us look forward to the future for better times. Those people think that they will be happier when they graduate from college or when they get married or when the kids are out of the house. They feel that everything will be fine when they retire. They seem to always be putting off the happy time for a future year or event.

The truth of the matter is that the present is the only time we have. We can be just as happy now as at any other time. Good and bad happen to everyone every day; our mood truly depends on what we are focusing our attention on now, in the present, at this moment. People are pretty much as happy as they make their minds up to be. We can decide to be happy today. In reality no one can live in the past or the future. They really do not exist. The past is just a memory, and even that memory is that which we choose to have of it in our minds now. There is nothing we can do to make the past any different then it actually was. What is done is done. What was said was said. What was thought was thought. If we want to do anything about the past we have to do it in the now. Even the choice to have nostalgic memories of the past is a choice that we make in the present. We routinely create and rearrange our memories in order to support our current thinking. I see this all the time when people fight and argue about events of the past. They will each have a different perspective or memory of the event which proves their point of view in the present situation. Memory is very selective. We remember events as we desire to remember them.

It is impossible to do anything in the future. We can only plan now for tomorrow and act when the future is the present. The past was actually filled with good and bad and the future will be filled with good and bad. It is our way of dealing with the events of life on a daily basis that makes the difference in our happiness. If a person can find unhappiness in their current condition, then it is likely that they will find unhappiness in the future also. It is not normal for someone to suddenly wake up one day with a different outlook on life. It is true that for a while the new job, or other change, will seem to fulfill all the requirements for happiness, but after a while the same types of problems which limited the person's ability to rejoice will again surface. Life is a constant string of problems and difficulties, the solutions to which are what allow us to grow and mature in the first place. The joy of solving problems and living in a creative manner is available for every situation in life. Joy and happiness are manifested despite problems, not because problems do not exist.

We are not our past. We are only that part of the past that we accept and keep in the now. We do not have to be our mistakes, we can be our successes. At any point we can decide to change our lives. We can leave our mistakes behind and make better decisions now. We can leave our prejudices behind and start loving now. We can leave our materialism behind and start being more spiritual. All our attitudes and mannerisms are habits that we have established which may be reshaped each and every moment. Our habits are behaviors which we repeat over and over in an automatic way. At any moment we may decide to change our choices and make new or different habits.

We are not our future either. I may say that someday I will be a doctor, but unless I do something now about it that someday will never come. I may have an idea for a book, but unless I sit down now and actually write the book, it will never be created. Thinking, acting, feeling are all done today, this moment, this very instant. Living is only done now. The power is in the now. We can only learn from the past, plan for the future, and live in the present.

6. Law of Communication

We are all one with God and we all have the right to personal revelation from God. If we are one with God and God is one with us then we ought to be able to communicate with ourselves. Some people seem not to believe that God still communicates with man. They acknowledge that God talked with people anciently. In the Bible, Torah, Qur'an and almost all books of ancient spiritual wisdom God is portrayed as communicating commonly with people. Moses talked with God and received commandments directly from Him. Mohammed received revelation from the angel Gabriel. Ezekiel received visions from God. People today clearly believe that at some point God did communicate with man, but often seem reluctant to admit that God still has this capacity today. It is okay for God to speak anciently, but not in modern times. This seems very foreign to me because all around me, and throughout my life, I see and hear evidence of God's communication to man. There is no reason why God is unable to communicate with us. He still lives. He has all of His godly powers. He still loves us. He is eternal and unchanging. It can only be our inability to receive His message that prevents communication. We are so caught up in the ways of the world that we ignore our spiritual development.

Many people pray to God expecting some form of answer to their prayer. Many of the answers they expect would imply that God would somehow communicate with them. They pray for wisdom in handling a difficult situation in their life. They ask for guidance and look for answers to questions. They pray for direction. I do not know how anyone can seriously pray for wisdom without expecting God to somehow communicate with them. Any communication from God is revelation. It does not matter how it is done, or what we personally call it. There are groups of people today that openly proclaim that God still talks to man. The members of The Church of Jesus Christ of Latter-day Saints believe in modern revelation both personally and through modern day prophets. Members of the New Age Movement believe that God speaks to all of us and psychics such as Edgar Cayce, Sylvia Browne, or Jane Roberts have a direct connection with spiritual beings. The Dali Lama is believed by many people to be God's mouth on earth. I believe God is all powerful and is still very much interested in mankind, as much today as in the past. I believe God continues to reveal helpful information to us on earth as a loving, benevolent Father trying to help His children. Men have certainly taken many of God's words of counsel and twisted them for their own selfish purposes, but that is man's doing, not God's doing. God will continue to do what He has always done in the past; to help, guide, and encourage all His children.

How does God communicate with us? There are many ways, and they all are included in the concept of revelation. Inspiration is probably one of the most common ways for God to communicate, yet many people do not seem to take inspiration as real communication from a higher power. Most of what we have in scripture is inspired of God. People of all religions regard their personal canon of scripture as inspired by God by whatever name He is called. Men who receive revelations, or visions, and were inspired by the Holy Spirit to write it down were known as prophets, and the writings became scripture. The apostle John on the Isle of Patmos was given a vision from deity and he was inspired to write it down and it became the Book of Revelation in the Bible.

Mohammed received revelation through the angel Gabriel and wrote it down and it became the Qur'an. Joseph Smith was inspired to write down the meaning of ancient markings on metal plates and it became the Book of Mormon. Moses received visions on the top of Mount Sinai and was inspired to write them down and it became the Pentateuch. Scriptures are inspired writings.

We as individuals receive inspiration also. This is such a common experience that we discount it, but it is just as much communication from God as if an angel came down and stood before us. The problem is that every time anyone has declared that they have received inspiration from God, they have been mocked and persecuted. We have learned to hide this form of revelation and deny its source in an effort to avoid personal ridicule and persecution. It is not socially acceptable in today's world to declare that God has spoken. People say the information came from their subconscious. Maybe our subconscious is merely our connection with the infinite universal energy field to which we all contribute, including God. We just are not openly declaring that we have received information from outside of our self. We all need to give God more credit than we do. He can and does talk to each of us frequently and we need to start acknowledging His communication in ourselves and others. Inspiration occurs when we receive a novel thought in our conscious mind. We often recognize that the thought came from outside of ourselves and it often is accompanied by strong feelings of truth or divinity. If acted upon, the inspiration will lead to a beneficial outcome.

One reason why people may not want to acknowledge inspiration as communication from God is the belief that only crazy people hear voices inside their heads. I am not talking about hearing voices, but about receiving new ideas and thoughts. We have all experienced the sudden occurrence of an idea which seemed to originate from outside of our consciousness. The sudden burst of insight is the inspiration of which I write.

Another way that God talks to us is through dreams. Often when we are struggling with a difficult situation we will have a vivid dream that helps us to understand the solution to our problem. Dreams have inspired new inventions, artistic works, movies and plays. Dreams have taught us the nature of God and details of the spiritual realms. Dreams have been recorded in the scriptures. The Old Testament relates that Daniel and Joseph of Egypt, among many others, interpreted important dreams that spoke of future events. Many of us have had important dreams that influenced our decisions and actions.

Many people make it a habit of spending a few minutes each morning upon awakening of remembering and paying attention to their dreams. Some people even keep a dream journal and take the time to write down and analyze their dreams. Everyone dreams, but unless we are consciously focused on our dream upon awakening, it will not be imprinted into our long term memory. It will quickly fade as we go about our daily activities.

Other less common ways of revelation are angelic visitations, an audible voice from heaven, and visions from God. All of these methods are clearly documented in the Bible. I know personally that God communicates to people because He communicates to me. I have heard His audible voice giving me warning and direction. I had visions where I was comforted in time of need. I have been inspired over and over again in my life and the writing of this book is in direct response to inspiration from God. I was even publicly ridiculed when I declared direction from God in my professional life. The disbelief of others can never take away from me the fact that God has, does, and will communicate with me. I am really no one special, no more special than any one else. I know that if I receive direction from God, anyone can receive similar communication. We are all one. We are one with God.

People who deny that they receive revelation from God usually are not recognizing the spiritual direction for what it is. Sometimes I think of the radio analogy. There are radio waves all around us all the time. We all know that in order to be able to hear those waves we need a device, a radio, that can receive those waves and change them into sounds that we can hear. A person who does not have a radio or is ignorant of the concept of radios and radio waves may even doubt the existence of the radio waves. They may be dubious of the whole idea that we could use an instrument to convert invisible energy in the air into sounds that can be heard. If they are primitive and we turn on a radio they might think that we have magical powers. Even if we have a radio it might not be able to receive the radio waves if it has no electrical power, if we drop the radio and break it, or if we are not tuned into the same frequency or station as the radio waves.

The same is true for receiving communication from deity. We all have the instrumentation for receiving communication from God built into each and every one of us. It is our part of our nervous system, and it is a very sensitive instrument which must be developed. Just as our muscles need exercise to work their best, our divine receiver needs exercise to be strengthened. At birth we all have the ability to hear God's voice. As we develop through the years our ability to receive inspiration is dependent on the attention we give to this inspiration. Just as muscles atrophy and weaken if unused, our divine receiver atrophies if we ignore spiritual insights. At any time we may start to exercise and thereby strengthen our muscles. At anytime we may start to seek and pay attention to communication from God and begin to strengthen our divine receiver.

Some of the advice about health from God has to do with His recommendations on how to keep the nervous system well tuned and able to receive revelation and inspiration. Some of the medications and drugs common in society today chemically alter the brain and change our ability to hear God. I often need to take morphine for a chronic pain disorder and I notice that it is much harder for me to feel the inspiration from God when I take the morphine. If I can reduce the morphine for a few days then the connection with God becomes more evident. Some people have found that certain chemicals improve their ability to connect with the spirit. Life is very strenuous for some people and their nervous system gets out of balance. Chemical imbalances leading to depression, anxiety, and other nervous disorders is very well known in medicine, and many excellent medications, chemicals, are produced to combat such conditions. When people rely on these medications for their emotional stability it may well help them to meditate and receive spiritual information. Mind altering substances have been used throughout history to augment and encourage divine information and to liberate an individual's creativity. We certainly live in a world very different from our ancestors' and our nervous systems have not had the time to genetically adjust to the rapid changes in civilization. There is no dishonor in the judicious use of these neurological chemicals if they help the individual. I believe that it is extremely important for each of us to learn for ourselves how to best "tune in" to the spirit of divine inspiration. We each need to strengthen our own spiritual muscles.

Instruction about the manner of communicating with God is widely available. Sages throughout the ages have tried to show us the way to inspiration and personal spirituality. Often their words of wisdom are misinterpreted and used for argument and contention instead of advice on ways to connect with God. There are probably as many ways to communicate with God as there are people. God wants to talk to all of us; He is not in the habit of excluding anyone. He loves us all and we are one. These are some of the steps I have found helpful in my life.

Study the matter in your mind.
Ponder and meditate on the scriptures.
Inquire of God in faith with an honest heart.
Be open to communication from God.
Live according to your understanding of God.
Be meek and humble.
Focus on the things of God.

1. Study the matter in your mind.

In order to be prepared to receive an answer to our problems from God we often need to be involved with the solution. It is important to think and learn about the various aspects of the problem before we try to find answers. This life is one of learning and growing, and one thing that we all need to learn is how to solve problems and come to conclusions by ourselves. God is not our personal genie, there to provide us our every whim. God allows us to struggle a bit. It is similar to helping one of our children with a homework assignment. Instead of just doing it for them without any work on their own, we usually encourage the student to research answers, read the book, refer to class notes, and so forth so that the child will learn from the experience. This earth life is like a school, we are learning to be like God. The struggle that we face in researching the answers to our own problems in life makes us each stronger and more able to function in a godlike manner. For instance, if we needed to decide which of two jobs would be in our best interest to take, we would find out about both jobs, the pros and cons of the employ before turning to God for an answer. Often in the process of researching the answer we come to a conclusion and feel that a certain decision is correct for us. The process of working and struggling with a problem will often result in a moment of clarity or inspiration, a "eureka" moment when the solution becomes apparent. These solutions and ideas may even seem to originate within ourselves, but it is really God in action. After all, we all are one, and we are one with God. Some people say that it is the god inside of them that revealed the answer, but it is still inspiration "from God".

Nikola Tesla, the father of our current AC electrical system struggled to find a way to efficiently run electrical motors on alternating current. He pondered various ideas for years until one day in 1882 during a walk at sunset, "The truth was suddenly revealed." In a few weeks Tesla was able to work our virtually all the types of induction motors and the electrical system to drive them that we still use to this day. (Seifer, Marc J., *Wizard The Life and Times of Nikola Tesla Biography of a Genius,* Kensington Publishing Co., 1998, pp. 22-23)

2. Ponder and meditate on the scriptures.

Reading and studying scriptures is an important aspect of revelation from God. The scriptures, as inspired writings from God, help us understand the spirit of God and the manner in which God has inspired men in the past. Seeing the pattern of revelation in the lives of others helps us to see the same pattern in our own lives. Often when we are reading and meditating about the scriptures we will gain insight into our own life or problems. The scriptures tend to put our minds in tune with the spirit of God in the same way that turning the dial on a radio tunes in to a certain station. When we ponder the things of God, our minds become more tuned to the voice of God. This is true for other activities also, for instance, if we listen to popular music with a heavy musical beat we feel more like getting up and dancing. If we watch a horror movie by ourselves in the middle of the night we are more likely to become afraid of the noises of the night. We respond to the mood of the environment around us, to the energy to which we are exposed. When we read and study and meditate on the things of deity, we are more likely to be in a mood where we may receive the spirit of revelation and inspiration.

3. Inquire of God in faith with an honest heart.

This is usually done in a prayer or similar meditative activity. Prayer is communication with God. When we pray sincerely to a higher power, or God, we open up the lines of communication with deity. Prayer can take many forms. Some people recite prayers taught them in church, such as the Lord's Prayer. Some people pray at certain times, prostrating themselves on a special tapestry, and facing towards a special direction. Some pray before altars with candles or incense burning. Some pray vocally with many ornate words, others pray silently with simple expressions of emotion. There are probably as many ways to pray as there are people. It is the emotion behind the prayer activity which gives it power. God responds to our intent and sincerity. The words we say matter much less than the intensity of our thought and the strength of our emotion. Our thoughts generate the spiritual field which spreads throughout the universe and our emotions give energy or power to that signal. God responds to each and every prayer.

There is no "right" way to pray, each must find the way that feels right to them. There is really only what works and what does not work. If you have been taught a way to pray and it works for you, then you know the joys of Godly communication and you will continue in this most intimate personal relationship. If prayers seem more like words that do not go beyond the confines of your room then do not despair, I promise that God is aware of your sincere efforts and will respond to you at the right place and time for you. Be patient and keep experimenting to find your personal way of praying and communicating with God. Do not be afraid to try new ideas and be open for direction from within. Express yourself openly to God, He knows you personally and you are not going to deceive Him or be something you are not. You must always be truly sincere.

In *The Adventures of Huckleberry Finn,* Huck says: "It made me shiver. And I about made up my mind to pray; and see if I could not try to quit being the kind of boy I was, and be better. So I kneeled down. But the words wouldn't come. Why wouldn't they? It warn't no use to try and hide it from Him. Nor from *me,* neither. I knowed very well why they wouldn't come. It was because my heart warn't right; it was because I warn't square; it was because I was playing double. I was letting *on* to give up sin, but away inside of me I was holding on to the biggest one of all. I was trying to make my mouth *say* I would do the right thing and the clean thing. But deep down in me, I knowed it was a lie,- and He knowed it. You can't pray a lie - I found that out." (Twain, Mark, *The Adventures of Huckleberry Finn,* Mark Twain Foundation, University of California Press, 2001, pg. 269)

God will respond to us according to our true desires and needs. When we make a consistent effort to pray, we place ourselves in an emotional state where communication with God is more likely. When we turn on a radio we can more easily hear the music than if we never bothered to turn the radio on in the first place. It might take some practice with the radio, turning it on and searching the channels until we are able to receive the message from the person or station with which we desire to communicate. Learning to communicate with God may take time and effort. Communication from God is worth the effort, both today and tomorrow.

4. Be open to communication from God.

Prayer implies revelation. When we pray, we expect God to somehow answer. We do not pray to dead idols who are incapable of hearing and understanding our prayers. We know that there is a power in the universe that directly understands our prayers and is very capable of responding. We need to be open to the idea that God will communicate with us. We need to be willing to hear and accept the word of God if we are ever going to receive answers to our prayers. Why would God respond to us if we were not going to listen to His response? Can you imagine asking God what job to take and then ignoring His answer when He gives it to us? Sometimes we may not like the answer that God gives; sometimes my children do not like the answer that I give them when they ask me for something. It is always unwise to seek for answers from God to our questions and then ignore the answer. I have personally prayed consistently for most of my life and have had many experiences which I directly attribute to God answering my personal prayers. I have encountered many people throughout my life who have told me stories of how God answered their prayers. It is not unexpected that God would respond to our attempts at communication with Him. The scriptures of almost every religion tell of God's interest in mankind and ways in which He communicates with humans. We truly are not alone in the universe, and each of us has access to a source of perfect wisdom and understanding. What surprises me most is how many people seem to find it unusual that God would talk to man.

The New Age movement started because of one man, Edgar Cayce, who was able to dictate in trance state the words of a higher power. This phenomenon seemed so uncommon that many people started seeking out Mr. Cayce's source of wisdom for their own problems. The fact that these question and answer sessions were recorded and documented allows them to be studied and they became the basis for wisdom and teaching in this movement. This work was furthered in the 1960's and 1970's with more spiritual material received and then published by Jane Roberts, Helen Schucman, and others.

In the 1990's Neale Donald Walsch called out to God in despair and anguish and was shocked and surprised to hear God's answer as a voice within his mind. He wrote these words from God and they became a series of books entitled *Conversations with God, an uncommon dialogue*. We should not be surprised that God answered Mr. Walsch's sincere desire for godly instruction. God is close to all of us when we are ready to receive God's wisdom.

Society seems surprised when God speaks today. We struggle with and anguish over the problems we face but cannot seem to believe that God can and will talk to us, personally. We have been instructed by our churches that revelation stopped 2000 years ago and that God no longer talks to man. If we would reflect on our personal lives we would know without doubt that God still talks because we have heard His voice. Most of us doubt when we hear Him and pass it off as our imagination, because of course, God does not talk today. Well, He does talk, and we need to listen and celebrate the joy of God talking to us. The problems of society and the world will continue for as long as we deny the power of God and refuse to seek Him. Think about how wonderful life would be if everyone heard the voice of God and used God's wisdom in searching for solutions to life's problems. Instead of looking toward some ecclesiastic authority we each would look towards God Himself.

Moses stated this desire in the Old Testament. The nation of Israel had left Egypt and crossed the Red Sea and they were being instructed by God on Mount Sinai. "So Moses left the Tabernacle and reported Jehovah's words to the people; and he gathered the seventy elders and placed them around the Tabernacle. And the Lord came down in the Cloud and talked with Moses, and the Lord took of the Spirit that was upon Moses and put it upon the seventy elders; and when the Spirit rested upon them, they prophesied for some time.

But two of the seventy—Eldad and Medad—were still in the camp, and when the Spirit rested upon them, they prophesied there. Some young men ran and told Moses what was happening, and Joshua (the son of Nun), one of Moses' personally chosen assistants, protested, "Sir, Make them stop!"

But Moses replied, "Are you jealous for my sake? I only wish that all of the Lord's people were prophets, and that the Lord would put his Spirit upon them all!"" (Numbers 11:24-29)

When we seek communication from God, He responds. He is always there, waiting and watching for us to start trying to communicate with Him. When we are sincere, He is close by. A prayer opens the lines of communication. God does not change from one generation to the next. He is just as capable of answering prayer now as He was yesterday, last year, last century, or anciently. It is up to us to be open to hear the words that flow from God into our lives.

5. Live according to your understanding of God.

The next step in receiving revelation from God is to live according to the understanding of God and from God that we have. If we pray and receive messages from God we should follow those messages. If we have religious beliefs, we should live our religion. Of course, no one is perfect, but we need to be doing our best and not ignoring the principles that we have personally received. God's purpose in communicating with us is to help us change our lives for the better. His purpose is to enlighten us and help us to progress in our journey towards perfection. Opening the door of revelation from God changes everything. It changes the way we perceive life, the way we think, the way we feel, and our relationships with others with whom we live.

God will never give someone more information than he is ready to start to live. When the student is ready the master appears. What is the use of revealing ways to cure disease through stem cell research if we are not going to use the information? What is the use of revealing healthful eating habits if we are still going to gorge ourselves to obesity? Why reveal the nature of God if we are going to use the information to fight with and destroy others who do not believe the way we do?

Personal revelation is for our personal use. Information is given to us for our own growth and understanding, not to use to harm and judge others. It is alright that there is diversity of human behavior in this world. God allows each of us the right to worship whom, what, or how we desire; we need to give that right to others around us and in the world. We need to understand that our way is not the only way to live and worship God. There are as many ways as there are people on earth. Each person on earth has the right to find the way to worship that is best for him. Who are we to say that what works for us is better than what works for them? If it works, keep on worshipping. If it does not work, then read, study, ponder, and pray, and God will direct you in the way you should go. I have no doubt that God is able to inform anyone who sincerely seeks Him that He exists and will direct that person in the way that is best for them. Instead of killing others because they are heathens or infidels, we should live our personal lives according to the way we believe. We can have a great influence for good in the world if we will do this.

Christ taught, "You are the world's seasoning, to make it tolerable. If you lose your flavor, what will happen to the world? And you yourselves will be thrown out and trampled underfoot as worthless. You are the world's light—a city on a hill, glowing in the night for all to see. Don't hide your light! Let it shine for all; let your good deeds glow for all to see so that they will praise your heavenly Father." (Matthew 5:13-16)

This is the only proper way to teach and lead others, by example. Do we give lip service to the adage "love one another" but then treat our neighbor like enemies? Do we listen and try to understand, or do we get angry and try to prove our righteousness? When the disciples of Christ were arguing about which of them was greatest, Christ taught that the greatest would be the one that served the others. Loving others means serving others. Teaching someone means serving that person. Healing the sick entails service to them. Service is the great key of life that allows us to demonstrate our love for others and our understanding of God's nature. God shows love through service to us. We emulate God when we serve others, be it our spouse, our children, our co-workers, our neighbors, the nation around the world from us.

6. Be meek and humble.

Meekness and humility are traits which are essential if one is to receive revelation. Meekness does not mean weakness. Humility is not self-depreciation. Humility and meekness are attitudes which are essential to learning. We have to realize that we do not know everything before we can be taught. I use the words humility and meekness as synonyms indicating a patient and submissive attitude before God. We must realize that as humans we are all equal and one person is not inherently greater than another. We all are dependent on God for everything especially for spiritual knowledge. Christ is the perfect example of meekness and humility. He became fully one with God and was able to act in full accord with His perfect submission to God's will. He was meek and humble before the Father even while casting the money changers out of the temple.

Humility implies an understanding that God is greater than we are. Our humility and desire for knowledge is what allows us to seek for answers in the first place. Someone who thinks they know it all is very difficult to teach. Some of these people are so resistant to learning that they close their minds to any new information. We are often like these people when it comes to spiritual matters. We believe the simple stories with which we were indoctrinated as children and we do not even realize that there is so much more of which we are not even aware. It is only when we admit that we are not all knowledgeable, that there are things about God, humans, and the eternities that we do not understand that we start on the quest for spiritual knowledge. Every thinking self aware person must at some point in his life ponder the big questions, who am I, where did I come from, why am I here, where am I going? We are only able to learn when we are open to learning. The student has to be ready before any teaching can occur.

The path to spiritual wisdom is the same as the path to secular wisdom. We research what others have written, we study the subject matter, we make theories, and we perform experiments to test our theories. We must constantly reevaluate what we believe to be true and make sure it is consistent with the results of our research. In order to receive wisdom from God, we have to be willing to listen, willing to be taught, willing to give up our old theories if they do not fit with the information coming through inspiration. Our personal pride can greatly limit our quest for truth.

I remember years ago when I used to argue with people about interpretations of the Bible. (Not a very good activity, I found that it is impossible to "prove" my perceptions to someone else, they have to go to God for their answers, just as I have to go to God for my answers.) The man became irate that something I taught him could be supported by scripture and in frustration took that page in his Bible and ripped it out stating, "My Bible does not say that!"

Often we will resist new ideas just because they are contrary to our personal belief system. We feel threatened by new ideas. For example, psychologists sometimes refer to "past life regression" therapy to help people through difficulties. It has been demonstrated many times that people have in their subconscious minds memories of other lives which can be accessed through hypnosis. I personally believe that we pass through this earth life only once. I can only deal with this discrepancy by either accepting the new information that people can come to earth multiple times or figure out some other spiritual insight that explains the phenomenon of past life regression. This gives me the opportunity to learn and grow spiritually; I must turn to God for the resolution of this problem because I do not know what is true. Instead of threatening us, new ideas should stimulate us to learn, think, study, and grow.

Traditionally religion has dealt with new ideas by blaming them on the devil. A prophet teaching unpopular doctrine would be accused of doing the devil's work. Mohammed's experience was explained by many as a visitation from Satan and not an angel. Edgar Cayce and other psychics today are sometimes accused of being guided by evil spirits who want to deceive us. Even Jesus Christ was accused by the Jews of the day of performing miracles by the power of Satan. By keeping an open mind to new ideas and information we are able to learn and grow spiritually. Eventually my personal theories of spirituality have to take second place to information I receive through revelation and inspiration from God. Unless I acknowledge that God is smarter and more knowledgeable than I, it is unlikely I will ever receive answers to my questions or direct personal revelation from God.

7. Focus on the things of God.

Finally, it is essential that we focus on the things of God and not on the things of the world. This has to do with our motivation to learn and seek help from God in the first place. Are we attempting to develop an alternate fuel source for personal profit and gain? Are we trying to win the Nobel Prize? Do we seek after the acclaim of the world, to become one of the "rich and famous"? Or is it our nature to give of ourselves for the benefit of others? Whose praise do we seek, God's or Man's? If we are to grow spiritually and seek for wisdom from God we need to be focused on what God wants. What does God want? Nothing. Nothing for Himself. He loves us. He is perfect all by Himself. He needs nothing from us. He tells us, "For behold, this is my work and my glory—to bring to pass the immortality and eternal life of man." (Moses 1:39) This is how we should be. We should want nothing for ourselves. Our motivation for doing well and accomplishing amazing tasks should be our love for others and our desire to help mankind. If we seek to help others, if we seek to love God then God will respond to our good and loving desires. God knows all the things that we need and want. He knows the desires of our hearts. He will provide for us in every way imaginable if we first seek Him and His righteousness.

In the Old Testament God appeared to King Solomon and offered the king anything he desired. Solomon asked for wisdom and knowledge, so that he could be a good and wise king and serve the people of Israel well.

God replied, "Because your greatest desire is to help your people, and you haven't asked for personal wealth and honor, and you haven't asked me to curse your enemies, and you haven't asked for a long life, but for wisdom and knowledge to properly guide my people—yes, I am giving you the wisdom and knowledge you asked for! And I am also giving you such riches, wealth, and honor as no other king has ever had before you! And there will never again be so great a king in all the world!" (2 Chronicles 1:11-12)

King Solomon had the right attitude. It is this type of thinking that we need to encourage in our own lives. Jesus taught, "So don't worry at all about having enough food and clothing. Why be like the heathen? For they take pride in all these things and are deeply concerned about them. But your heavenly Father already knows perfectly well that you need them, and he will give them to you if you give him first place in your life and live as he wants you to.

So don't be anxious about tomorrow. God will take care of your tomorrow too. Live one day at a time." (Matthew 6:31-34)

We really do not need to worry about ourselves, we need to be about our Father in Heaven's business of helping others and the universe will take care of all of our personal needs. When we are focused on the work of loving God and loving our neighbor the channel of communication from God is strengthened. It helps us to tune in to God's spirit or voice when we are thinking about God's work of divine love.

I need to clarify myself a little. I just said that we should want nothing for ourselves. That is the attitude that we need to cultivate within ourselves. Of course we do need things for ourselves, and the universe will allow us to receive all the things we need. It is the attitude of putting God first, others second, and ourselves third that I am trying to emphasize. We need to work towards the greater good of all and not just selfishly think of ourselves. We live in a physical world and it is the nature of this world to require that we sustain ourselves in order to survive. If we go without food or water very long we will become too weak to be of any service to anyone and we may eventually die, cutting short our opportunity to learn and grow as much as we are able while living here on this earth plane. Adam was commanded by God to labor for his own sustenance. "…All your life you will sweat to master (the soil), until your dying day." (Genesis 3:19)

It is important for us to be able to take care of ourselves and those of our families for whom we are responsible. It is important to be able to pay our bills and learn to take care of our earthly needs. Our spirits need nothing, but our physical bodies need to be cared for. Once we have enough to take care of ourselves, we need to be looking around us to see the needs of those with whom we come in contact. We need to give generously to those in need and use our resources for doing good in the community. The good that we do needs to be done because we love others, not because we expect God to give us something because of our good behavior. The universe is aware of our true intentions and we need to keep our thoughts and actions pure in order to progress spiritually and receive further light and knowledge from the heavenly source.

CHAPTER V
PEACE ON EARTH

1. Stop Fighting

Everyone has the ability to choose for themselves what to believe. It is impossible to legislate morality. A person freely chooses the convictions and the principles to direct their own life. Forcing someone to believe or to think a certain way is commonly known as brainwashing and is considered an extreme misuse of human relationships and victimization of the person so controlled.

Everyone has their own path to follow in this life. Even God does not interfere with personal choice; He gives all mankind free agency and free will. Free will means just that, the ability to make one's own decisions. The war in heaven (if you believe in such stuff) seems to have been centered on issues of free agency, God wanted men to be free to choose, and Satan wanted to force all people to do what He wanted. (See Moses 4:1-4 in *Pearl of Great Price,* by Joseph Smith, The Church of Jesus Christ of Latter-day Saints, 1996) Why would any person professing religious beliefs and pursuing a life of "loving others as himself" or "doing unto others as you would have others do to you" ever want to interfere with another person's freedom of belief? If God really "wanted" or "needed" every person to bow down and worship Him, He could easily manifest Himself in some Mighty Way and convince the "infidels" that HE IS. This is not the way of God and this is not the way of spirituality. It is fine to declare one's own beliefs, but it is never appropriate to force one person's belief on another. Force leads to violence and bloodshed; and there has been way too much of that over the years, all in the name of religion. The religious statements that every knee shall bow and every tongue confess that Jesus is the Christ, that Allah is God, or that Jehovah is the Lord, are not invitations to force all mankind to worship our way or to kill those who refuse to bend the knee. They are statements of the eternal truth that eventually every person, sometime in the eternities, in this life or another, on earth or in the spirit world will know that God exists and is an exalted being worthy of reverence and emulation. We will see Him as He is, and we will all realize that we are like Him. (See 1 John 3:2) We are all one, we are one with God.

Is it our inherit nature to love and serve others or to love and serve ourselves? I think that the bigger issue is that either way, it does no one good here in this life or in the life to come to argue, fight, and destroy other people just because we have diversity of belief. I personally believe that there is still much to learn, and that by gaining a personal relationship with God, a person may tap into the only source of true knowledge that exists. Anything less than pure personal revelation from God is just some man's opinion. We can always respect that person's opinion, but we do not have to fight about it. Talk to God about your ideas and God will talk back to you.

Christ taught, "The law of Moses says, "If a man gouges out another's eye, he must pay with his own eye. If a tooth gets knocked out, knock out the tooth of the one who did it." But I say: Don't resist violence! If you are slapped on one cheek, turn the other too. If you are ordered to court, and your shirt is taken from you, give your coat too. If the military demand that you carry their gear for a mile, carry it two. Give to those who ask, and don't turn away from those who want to borrow.

There is a saying, "Love your friends and hate your enemies." But I say: Love your enemies! Pray for those who persecute you! In that way you will be acting as true sons of your Father in heaven. For he gives his sunlight to both the evil and the good, and sends rain on the just and on the unjust too. If you love only those who love you, what good is that? Even scoundrels do that much. If you are friendly only to your friends, how are you different from anyone else? Even the heathen do that. But you are to be perfect, even as your Father in heaven is perfect." (Matthew 5:38-48)

If America has so many Christians, and they profess to follow Christ, then why do we have so much contention in America? Why is there so much crime? Why is divorce so common? Why is violence taught so forcefully in the media and in so many video games? Why do children rise up against parents, and parents abuse their children? We all need to start living our personal beliefs instead of arguing about who is right.

There is a method of resolving conflict that I call the cookie cure. When there was a neighbor that seemed particularly irritable and caustic I would try to find nice things to do for that neighbor, like take them cookies. I found that the more I did in service to that neighbor, the happier the neighbor seemed and often the problems with fighting in the neighborhood would lessen. I would usually choose the least liked neighbor, the one with the noisy kids and messy yard, the one who always yelled obscenities or got in fights. I pulled weeds for them, baked them brownies, took their kids on bike rides, mowed their lawns, lent them tools, and just was a friend, even if they still yelled and fought and continued to act out. Over time I noticed that these people would seem to calm down, and they often confided with me about their own problems. They would usually have good reasons in their mind why they acted like they did. They often believed that everyone hated them and life was terrible and that others mistreated them in some obscure way. Some people changed in response to my kindness, some people did not, but in any case I felt better about the person and understood them a little more. Instead of participating in the contention of the neighborhood, I exercised my freedom to live according to my belief that I should love my neighbor as myself. I do not have to expect anyone else to love their neighbor; I just have to be true to my own personal belief that I love my neighbor as myself. I did not have to convince any of my other neighbors to act in a like manner, they could still commiserate among them selves about the "bad" apple on the street, all I had to do was to live my own convictions.

Even in writing this book I am not expecting anyone else to believe what I believe or to do what I do, I am only expressing my viewpoints on life, and explaining to others what I have found to work for me in my life. Every one who reads this must decide for themselves what they want to believe and to disbelieve, how they wish to live their life or not live their life. People pretty much express what they truly believe by what choices they make in life. Instead of forcing others to act in a certain way it is better to teach them correct principles of life and allow them the freedom of choice. We do more good by living the laws of the universe that we understand than by trying to force someone else to do something in which they have no belief.

The universe is stranger than we can understand. I am the first to admit that I do not understand everything there is to know both physically and spiritually. I can only work hard to publish what I do know far and wide to try to teach and help mankind. We live in very perilous times. No time on the face of the world has there been so much war and potential to destroy our earth as in our modern times. In the past a person or nation had a limited ability to inflict harm on others. With the invention of weaponry far more dangerous than in past centuries one individual is able to inflict harm to millions of innocent people all across the world. I think back to the anthrax and small pox scares of the early 21st century. Of suicide bombers who use civilian airplanes as explosives such as the attacks of 9/11 on New York and Washington, D.C. I remember the bombs planted in areas of mass transportation in England which inflicted harm to innocent citizens.

We all need to learn to get along better with each other. Fighting and contention needs to stop. This begins with us, not with some one else. We need to stop bickering with our spouses and children. We need to learn to get along with our neighbors. We need to look to our workplaces and cities and towns and learn to do our jobs with an attitude of love and joy. If we start with ourselves, we can change the world. The key is to start. Work at it daily. Start praying to God. Mend our relationships with our parents and children. Start agreeing with those around us. Find common ground, celebrate our similarities. Smile. We need to admit that we do not have all the answers. We do not have the only way. We do not know everything. We need to stop trying to force others to believe the things we believe. What works for us may not work for them. We need to love others as ourselves. There really is not any them and us. We really are all one. We are all one with God.

We will only learn to get along with each other when we learn to live the first two laws of Christ, Love of God and Love of others. God sets an example of love for us. Godly love is called divine love. Divine love is a great and divine caring for others, a motivating power which inspires us to sacrifice for the well being of those we love, and a complete desire to bless others and serve others without seeking our own benefit. Divine love cannot exist in the midst of contention or in the attempt to control another person's belief.

Contention comes from the idea that there is not enough stuff to go around, not enough love, money, time, fame, or wisdom for everyone. We fight and argue in order to get our fair share. I sat in church recently and watched two young twins in the pew in front of me. They were well behaved for most of the meeting, but at one point one of them became somewhat fussy and his older sister gave him her cell phone to look at and with which to play. He was instantly fascinated with it, opening it and pushing the buttons. The other twin was immediately interested and quickly tried to grab it away from the first. A small scuffle ensued which had to be resolved by their mother.

It is often like that for each of us. We see something that we want. We see our neighbor drive up with their new car or boat. We walk through the store and see new electronic gadgets which attract our gaze. We watch the enticing advertisements on television. We see on the media the lifestyles and possessions of the rich and powerful and covet the things they have acquired. The myth of this life is that these things really mean something and that they are of limited supply, that there are not enough things for everyone. It is a myth that we do not have enough money for everything we desire. We become consumed with the attainment of material possessions which do not have any real meaning. Secular materialism has become the religion of the modern world. One hundred years from now it will probably not matter to anyone living today whether they drove a new Mercedes Benz car to work or drove an old Ford. The fact of the matter is that the things that are eternally important are in plentiful supply to all people who live here on earth. It is a myth that we cannot have all the things we need here in this life because of our circumstance or some personal limitation. The truth is that every person creates their surroundings from the time they are born until the day they die. Many of the most difficult situations we have in life are actually created by ourselves, through improper understanding and use of the natural laws of the universe. These laws may be used by everyone equally to obtain what they desire. It is up to us to start consciously using these laws to obtain what we desire and to stop being jealous of others. We need to stop blaming others for our problems.

2. Personal Peace

When we came to this physical reality our minds became fragmented. It became necessary for the mind to interact with the physical body and attend to its needs. This led to an incessant stream of demands on the mind. The body's voice in our consciousness requires food, sex, pleasure, power, and instant gratification. Freud named this part of our consciousness the Id.

There is also an additional voice in our mind which encourages us to pursue the high ideals of society. This is often generated by the cultural interpretation of desirable behavior, such as honesty, morality, and religiosity. This was named the Super-Ego by Freud.

Part of our mind must decide on a minute by minute basis what to think and how to act. We repress one voice and encourage the other. We consider all the various demands on our time and ability and choose how we will live our life. This part of our mind is known as the Ego.

Often, these components of our mind are depicted as a devil on one shoulder telling us to do "bad" stuff and an angel on the other shoulder encouraging us to make the "right" decision. Good and bad, right and wrong are created from the tensions between the various aspects of our current state. The fact that we are spiritual beings residing in a physical dimension with complete freedom to act for ourselves creates internal conflict. This conflict is what causes the fragmentation of our mind and creates the Ego. The Ego is not created by God, it is not eternal, and it is not real. It is merely a fabrication by our minds to deal with the tension within us between our physical and spiritual realities. We think that we are our Ego, but we are not.

The Ego feels vulnerable because it is temporary. It was not created by God and so it is only part of this current reality and does not exist or continue with us in the afterlife. The Ego has knowledge of these things, and it hides the truth from us. It knows that we are eternal children of God. It knows that we will always exist in God's good graces, that we are loved by God as children are loved by a perfect Father. The Ego knows that it is a temporary illusion of this earth life. It knows that it will not survive our death. We will survive, it will not. We are eternal, it is ephemeral. It is the Ego which fears death. Our death is its death. Our passing is its passing. Our fear of death comes from the Ego's fear of death. Our feelings of vulnerability come from the Ego's vulnerability.

The Ego comments on and judges everything we do. It often makes us feel guilty for our actions and berates our behavior. It is really making us feel guilty for having left the eternal realms of God in the first place. The Ego is the creator of our guilt, and the source of our inner desire for punishment. We have within each of us an enemy who hates us and desires our suffering and misery. It wants to punish us over and over again for separating ourselves from God.

We often listen more to what the Ego tells us about our existence than what our intuition tells us or the Spirit of God tells us. We believe what the Ego says because we do not realize that the Ego is our enemy. It only wants to punish us for having eternity when it does not. It is jealous of us and wants us to suffer.

We are the ones who create the Ego. Subconsciously we believe God will punish us because we separated ourselves from Him. That feeling of guilt rests deep within ourselves and is part of the tension that contributes to the creation of the Ego. The Ego then encourages us in ways that will always end up in creating our own suffering. We punish ourselves. We often define our existence by our suffering. We create drama in our lives because we feel we do not deserve to be happy and to be at peace. We tend to remember the painful experiences of life instead of the pleasant ones. We create a hell for ourselves because we think that God wants us in hell.

None of this thinking is factual. God does not want us to suffer. He loves us. He wants us to be happy and to join with Him. He continually sends His Spirit to help us and to remind us of the truth. We are not here on earth alone. We never really separated ourselves from God. We really are still very connected to God and separation is merely an illusion. Our separation from God and the creation of the Ego within us are both illusions of this dimension. Some day we will open our mind and realize that we have been mistaken in this earth life. We will see through the illusions and find ourselves in God's presence once more. God sends His Spirit to each of us to remind us that we are one with Him. When we listen to the voice of His Spirit and ignore the voice of the Ego we draw closer to God and see reality more like God sees reality. God's reality is that we are all one. The Spirit of God shows us this truth.

There are only two emotions, love and fear. God teaches love, the Ego teaches fear. All other emotions are just variations on these two. Anxiety is fear that something will hurt us now. Depression is fear that pain and suffering have no end. Jealousy is fear of not being able to obtain something we need or want. Happiness is love of life as it is now. Joy is love's expression. God wants only to bless us with feelings of joy, happiness, and peace. He does not wish our suffering. The Ego encourages the suffering. God is eternal and all powerful. The Ego is temporary, weak, and miserable. To listen to the Spirit is to find joy and love. To listen to the Ego is to find punishment.

The best way to tell if we are listening to the Spirit of God is to see how well we love. Forgiveness is the way we show our love for God, ourselves, and others. When we love ourselves, we forgive ourselves. We realize that we do not need to be punished for anything. Forgiveness takes away any need for retribution. If we forgive ourselves for separating from God, we do not need to be punished for it. We are not guilty, we are forgiven. There is no "original sin", it is forgiven. We forgive ourselves for being who we are. We forgive ourselves for creating the Ego. We realize that it is alright for us to be human, to have flaws, to make mistakes. We do not need to be punished because we are forgiven from all of our imperfections.

We show love for others when we forgive those around us. When we love someone we forgive them of their faults. We look past their imperfections. Unconditional, divine love means unconditional forgiveness. We do not need to punish or harm others because we love and forgive them. We do not need to point out their errors to them, that is not loving. To dwell on errors and think about them only gives the mistake more power. It is best to let the error pass by without comment, let it go and forgive those who have wronged us. If we truly love then we will not even perceive that we have been injured.

We are currently divided within. We have the battle of good and bad within us, the battle between the Spirit and the Ego. The Ego demands our attention. The Spirit invites us to listen, but never demands anything from us. Now is the time to choose to listen to the Spirit and shun the judgmental voice of the Ego. Now is the time to start loving ourselves enough to put aside our internal conflict and join fully with the Spirit of God. When we forgive ourselves and others for all the wrongs we perceive and imagine, we lose the need to judge ourselves and others. When we routinely and consistently forgive ourselves and others around us, the Spirit of God will fill our hearts with peace and love. This is the basis of divine love that can only come through the gift of the Spirit of God. When we love, we allow the Spirit to come to us fully and guide us down our path through life. It will be a constant companion to us filling our hearts and minds with eternal beauty and harmony. The Spirit will direct us towards serenity and the divine reunion with God.

3. Family Peace

The family is the basic organizational unit of society. The family is the best place to start practicing the principles that encourage peace in society. We can improve the way we relate to each other at home and in society. We can learn to love our family members. The current way that we treat each other is causing too much conflict in the world and threatens the fabric of society and the world in which we live. The family is the best place to start to make improvements. It allows us to experience relationship principles in a limited environment. The same habits of living may then be spread to all of society and ultimately to the entire world. How can we love our enemy and treat them well unless we have learned to love our spouse and children and treat them well. The steps to world peace begin with making changes in the way we relate to our own family members. We may not believe that humanity is one, but we can easily see that the members of our immediate family are genetically related and should be bound together by the bonds of love. If we can practice forgiveness and peace promoting activities at home then the habits we make there become basic to our nature and we can improve the way we treat others we encounter in our community.

Much of the turmoil and grief we experience on a daily basis come from conflict between us and our spouses or significant others. I question the need for conflict in this relationship that is supposed to be based purely on love. No one is forced (or should be forced) to enter into an intimate living arrangement with anyone else, we do so of our own free will. Once the relationship is established, we are only bound to it by the promises we make, our continued love, and our desire to maintain that relationship. The love we have for another person motivates us to practice living peace promoting principles. It is always easier to treat someone we love as we would like to be treated. The balance of giving service and receiving service, helping and receiving help, forgiving and being forgiven, sharing and being shared with can be practiced on a daily basis. We know and understand the needs of our spouse better than anyone else and we are in the best position to fulfill those needs. Intimacy and long term relationships do not give permission to threaten, coerce, and force anyone to do anything; it only provides opportunity to give unconditional love. We are happiest when our spouse is happy. We are fulfilled when our spouse is fulfilled. It is alright if the wife makes more money than the husband; her success brings joy to the whole family. Both spouses work together for their mutual benefit.

My wife likes bubble gum, I like chocolate. Both are enjoyable and it is silly to argue about who is right. No! Bubble gum is best! No! Chocolate! Many of the arguments between spouses seem as silly as this. We need to take a step back and look at the bigger picture. It is okay for our spouse to have what they want. It is okay to agree that they are right. (Even if we really know that they are wrong. NO! CHOCOLATE IS BEST!!!) Life is supposed to be enjoyable, relax and have fun together.

What may work well for one family may not work for another because every one's needs and beliefs are different from ours; we all have a different style of living. With unconditional love, lack of judgment, open communication, a sincere attempt to help one another, the happiness and well being of both spouses may be assured. At the end of each day ask your spouse one question, "Is there anything I could have done better for you today?" Then close your mouth and open your heart and listen to the answer. Do not talk back and try to defend yourself. This is not time to start an argument. Just let your guard down for a bit and listen to what your spouse is telling you. When she is done talking, smile, tell her you love her and then do a better job the next day. Our job is to focus on our spouse and see that their needs are fulfilled each day. Force, control, threats, harsh language, blame, violence, and judgment do not convey feelings of unconditional love.

I am always amazed when I hear about the attempts some people make to try to force someone else to love them. Love can only be freely given, it cannot be coerced. A relationship cannot be maintained by threats. You cannot beat a person into loving you. I know of a woman who threatened and attempted suicide many times to coerce a man into marriage with her. The marriage was tempestuous and short lived. It was built on the foundation of threats and force instead of on the foundation of mutual love and respect. If your relationship is on shaky soil then today you may choose to start giving unconditional love to your spouse. They may or may not love you back, but unconditional love is not dependent on their attitudes or actions. You can always find something to love about your spouse and work to emphasize their positive points.

When children are involved the adult's role is to protect them from harm and danger while they grow towards adulthood. Part of that protection is to teach them about the world and how to best survive in it. We naturally teach what has worked for us in our lives, but it is important to recognize, especially as they approach adulthood, that our children are unique individuals. They are not our clones. They may find that what works for us does not work for them. Loving unconditionally is always the best way to handle a situation. Children, especially teenagers, often test the limits of love, pushing parents as far away as possible in an attempt to assert their own desires. The best way to handle any given situation is found when the parents are united in love and open communication exists between all family members. Seeking spiritual wisdom and communication from God will often provide parents with the tools useful for helping their children.

I have always respected my parent's unconditional love for myself and all of my siblings. I have certainly had my problems in life and have made many poor choices. My parents have always been there to love me and help me through the difficult times. I have seen them act in a similar loving way towards my brothers and sister as we all struggle through life. Having loving parents has been a blessing in my life and I try to give unconditional love to my children. Even if we were not loved as children, we may give the gift of unconditional love to our children.

The way to handle any particular situation is often complex and it may be difficult to choose which way is best. For example, if you found out your sixteen year old unmarried daughter is pregnant you now have many options on how to deal with the situation. You could have the fetus aborted. You could kick your daughter out of the house and make her deal with the pregnancy on her own. You could force her to marry the father of the baby. You could, in some countries, have her killed. You could help her raise the baby. You could have the baby adopted. There are many choices. The best thing to do depends on your relationship with your daughter and her desires. She is probably afraid and overwhelmed and needs help and encouragement. Love is best conveyed to our children by listening to and helping them.

There was a man who had never had a horse or even been around horses who married a woman who loved horses and owned many of them. One day in an attempt to impress his bride, he decided to go out into the pasture and teach a young colt how to be led. He figured it would be easy to do, he was bigger than the colt, he was smarter than the colt, and he knew more than the colt. He went out and stood in front of the colt, holding the lead. He pulled on the lead, and the colt pulled back. He pulled harder on the lead, and the colt pulled harder back, digging in with its hooves. He finally pulled so hard that the colt fell over. This scene was repeated several times until after a few minutes he had managed to teach the colt how to fall down. All he had to do was to stand in front of the colt, tug on the lead, and the colt would promptly fall down. His wife, who was watching him, suggested another way to teach the colt to follow on a lead. She had him take the lead and stand next to the colt and then start walking. The colt walked with him and was easily taught to be led.

Each of us is a lot like that colt. We often do not like being told what to do. Any parent who has had teenagers in the home know how resistant to suggestion humans can be. Even gentle suggestions on changing teenager behavior are often met with resistance. The more forceful these suggestions become, the more resistance is mounted by the individual. Power struggles are common when the parents attempt to force a child to do something they do not want to do. As adults we do not like having someone tell us what we should do. We like to make up our own minds and choose our own life's destiny. This inherent desire of self determination is part of our basic nature.

God has given each of us our freedom of choice, our free agency. It is given unto man to choose for himself what path he will follow. If God will not force anyone, why do we as people try so hard to force our children to conform to our personal way of life? We would do better to follow the example of God and inspire them but never force. Our love and friendship should never be based solely on their beliefs. I am constantly amazed when I hear of parents who estrange themselves from their children because the child chooses a different religion or life path than the parents. I know a mother who has a strong Christian background who tries to control her adult children on their choice of church to attend. Her petty attempts go so far as to deny her daughter the use of a car on a Sunday when the daughter's car was in the repair shop. The daughter could use the mother's car to go to the store, or run other trivial errands, but if the daughter wanted to go to her own church, the car was not available. This mother's attempts at control only weaken their relationship; she cannot possibly think that by force she can ever convince her daughter that her church is the "right" one to attend. Peace at home leads to peace in our children. When the family is at peace society will only benefit.

4. Community Peace

Doctrine of moral behavior is for personal use and benefit, not to be invoked on others. If you do not believe that people should work on Sunday, then do not work on Sunday. Do not impose your belief on the rest of society. What constitutes work for one person may be en enjoyable relaxation for another, such as gardening. The Jewish laws about the Sabbath at the time of Christ became so extensive that when Jesus healed the blind man on the Sabbath, he was accused of breaking the law. We cannot impose our religious decisions on the whole community. When I was actively practicing medicine, I often attended sick people in the hospital. I had strong feelings about honoring the Sabbath day and so I never charged for these Sunday visits, but instead donated my time in Christian service to the sick. I did not have to complain about being forced to work on Sunday. I did not have to petition for new laws. I just lived my personal life according to my convictions.

Civil punishment should never come from religious doctrines. That is the principle of separation of Church and State. No one should be forced to believe in a certain moral ethic. In nations where the civil code is taken directly from religious morals there is often a great loss of personal freedom. Large segments of the population become oppressed in the name of morals. Women, minorities, and people of other faiths often become second class citizens. Minor infractions may be met with cruel and life threatening punishment. God never intended for people to be punished for not believing or worshipping Him. He does not need our worship, He is perfect. The commandments and teachings of religion are for our own personal benefit. They are to help us live in joy and peace. We may feel obligated to proclaim our beliefs and share them with the world, but we may never harm anyone for not believing in our way. We are supposed to love others, remember? How can we love someone by harming them? How can we blow up someone in a loving manner? It has always amazed me how messed up religious thinking becomes when mixed with political aggression. In the Crusaders Hymn the words are all about love and healing yet the crusaders were out to kill the infidels. Unbelievable! Were they actually singing the words of the song while slashing away with their swords or just humming the tune? We cannot preach love and peace with one hand and dole out death and misery with the other. God does not work that way. We cannot work that way. God makes the sun shine on both the righteous and the sinner. He also tells us not to judge one another. We cannot tell right from wrong. There is no good or bad. There is only what we believe or do not believe and what works or does not work. It does not work to go about harming each other in God's name, we only harm ourselves. We are all one. We are one with God.

When we watch children on a playground, they sort themselves into groups. These groups are based on the social positioning of the children and the children's self interest. This is known as politics. What governs playground behavior are the rules and regulations imposed by teachers. Companies run pretty much like the playground; politics with rules and regulations imposed by supervisors. Countries are the same. A better way to organize a group is to move away from politics and regulations and self interest towards self rule and love for others. When people believe that we are all one then they will act in the best interest of the group. Their actions will not need to be imposed by an outside influence or force. They will be enabled to achieve their maximum potential because their best effort will bring the group the greatest gain and thus they will benefit personally. It is fine to be and act selfishly when the whole of the community is included in the sense of self. Best government is self government; people understand correct principles and govern themselves.

5. Religious Peace

Religion contributes more to world conflict than any other entity. It is a person's belief system that allows them to think that it is reasonable to attack another person or nation. We believe that someone else deserves to be punished or to die. Just look at the violence and conflict over the issue of abortion. People who are against abortion because they believe it is killing human life are willing to kill those who support and perform abortions. So it is okay to kill someone to stop them from killing fetuses. How does this make sense? In the conflict in the Middle East today Allah condemns killing, but it is okay to commit suicide if one can kill some infidels also. We allow killing to defend our beliefs and our way of life from an aggressive nation. We attack others to liberate them from oppression. We believe that our way is better than their way. Historically millions of people were forced into Christianity at the point of a sword. Today the militant Muslins are attempting to force the whole world to worship Allah. Force did not work for the Christians and force will not work today. Religions can only be involved with teaching, not forcing.

Religions really only deal with three issues. 1. They define the nature of God and the relationship between God and man. 2. They define the best way to live our lives, the way to peace and happiness in this life and in the eternities. 3. They define our condition in the afterlife. We each have the opportunity to study as many religious systems as we desire and follow the one that most appeals to us. Religions can only offer fellowship and they may withdraw that fellowship if someone does not desire to participate. Religions cannot dole out criminal punishments or take a person's life. If anything, a religion would want to prolong the life of a non-believer in the hope that eventually the person would repent and make peace with God. We would never want to hasten someone's demise, especially if we thought them to be a "sinner".

Religion deals with our personal relationship with God. If someone refuses to believe or have faith then forcing them to go through the motions of religious rituals and social customs will not endear them to deity and will not help them in this life or the next. Force cannot change a person's belief. Beliefs are a reflection of our education and our personal experience. Children are indoctrinated by their parents. As adults we have to choose to continue to believe as we did when we were children, or to modify our beliefs due to our personal increased knowledge and experience. Most adults use their childhood teachings as a springboard to develop and define their own personal belief system.

The search for truth is what motivates most of us to investigate our own and others' beliefs. Truth is the way things really are. Unfortunately, truth may be elusive and hard to define perfectly. For example, the nature of light may be described as both a particle and a wave, and both a wave and a particle simultaneously. Often different belief systems are describing different aspects of the same truth. Both systems may be accurate and true, but different from each other. Like the blind men describing an elephant, each arguing about their individual sensory experiences, we get glimpses into the eternities and believe we have the whole truth. We argue about the differences we have with each other instead of recognizing our common beliefs.

Religion often gets mixed up with man's philosophies. The way I approach life affects the way I interpret divine inspiration. If I have obsessive-compulsive tendencies, then I might ritualize my religious experience. The ritualistic acts of cleansing, counting, checking, repeating would make my life feel more secure. If I were in a leadership position in my church, these ritualistic activities might become indoctrinated. People have changed all religious beliefs over the centuries to fit their personal agenda and philosophy. Pure doctrine from God will always emphasize individual freedom and personal spirituality.

I believe that the best religions are based on direct revelation from God. This will allow the doctrine of the church to be flexible and change to reflect man's changing situation. It was devastating to the Catholic Church in the Renaissance Age when so much of the Church's doctrine was based on an erroneous view of the cosmos. When science showed discrepancies between scientific fact and Church doctrine, such as the earth not being the center of the universe, many people lost faith in the Church. Spiritual truth should not conflict with scientific truth. Both should give an accurate description of how things really are in the universe. False religion and false science may conflict. False religion and true science may conflict. True religion and false science may conflict. True religion and true science should agree and mutually support each other. Currently, the chasm between religion and science is bridged by the explanation that the two entities are describing different aspects of reality. Today science and religion are starting to close the gap between the material world and the spiritual. Science and religion are both starting to describe the connectedness of the universe.

Experiments involving human consciousness, random quantum effects, and the zero point field suggest that we have a greater influence on our environment than previously suspected. (See *The Field* by Lynn McTaggart, Harper Collins Pub., 2002) Many of the quantum theories of subatomic particles are finding application in biologic systems. The physical and biological laws of science have primarily been based on the work and theories of Isaac Newton of the 17th century. For hundreds of years our science was based on separateness. One particle is separate from another. The world is made up of tiny building blocks that operate in a discrete manner. This paradigm was shattered for subatomic particles by the theories of quantum physics in the early 20th century. Now quantum principles are being applied to biologic systems. Once all matter was viewed as discrete bits of material, now we realize that we are all energy, connected by the energy fields that permeate the universe. The universe was once viewed as a machine; we humans were merely complex mechanisms struggling for survival. We stood separate from the universe looking into it, trying to figure out how it worked. Now the universe seems more like a living organism, with humans an integral part of the entire cosmos.

We really are all one. We are one with each other, we are one with God. We need to stop fighting over our beliefs. Both the science of Newton and the science of Einstein have valid application in our world. The religions of Buddha and of Mohammed have validity. Both Christ and Confucius taught spiritual truths.

In this book I am not trying to tell you what to do, or how to live your life. I am trying to teach the wisdom that I have learned in my own life in order to help others find their own way in life. I believe that all adults must choose for themselves who and what they value and worship. I personally have found that when I seek God and attempt to personally live the morals that I value I feel better about myself and the world around me. I have learned that the only person who I can control or command is myself. I control myself and I love my neighbor. I believe that each of us has our own path to follow in life and what works for me may not work for you. I can only teach from my personal experience.

This book is about my way to peace and harmony with deity. This is one way; it is certainly not the only way. To everyone reading this book I say to take what rings true to you in your life and apply the principles to the best of your ability. When God inspires you to believe or feel something different from me then follow the inspiration you personally receive and live that to the best of your ability. We are all brothers and sisters here on earth; we all seek growth and wisdom, peace and prosperity. We do not need to argue about who is right about details of belief or who is wrong; who is closer to God and who is distant. It is not important to judge others and seek to vault ourselves over others. We are all one, and we are on this journey together. It makes much more sense to spend our time and effort in helping each other along the path of spirituality and wisdom.

6. National Peace

The purpose of religion is to allow a group of similar believing people to join together and strengthen one another. The purpose of government is to allow a group of different believing people to live together in peace and harmony. The laws of a nation must allow freedom of thought and a diversity of belief. It is impossible to legislate a person's beliefs. Educating citizens is fine, it is even acceptable to teach a state religion, but rights of citizenship cannot be connected to a particular belief system. We live in a world that allows travel between nations and allows a diversity of culture throughout the world. Nations can no longer be based on common religious beliefs, but must be organized on geography and a sense of national unity and pride. It is unfortunate when citizens are punished because they do not believe the same way as their neighbor. If we take the attitude of "do unto others as you would have done unto you", we would afford others the opportunity to express their religious convictions just as we ourselves would like to have our beliefs tolerated if we were living in a foreign setting. We certainly do not need to embrace the beliefs and lifestyles of people different from ourselves, but we do need to tolerate their lifestyles and belief system. We need to stop being so judgmental. Punishment based on what someone believes only punishes ourselves. We are one. We are one with God.

7. World Peace

Throughout the ages humans have looked for a time when God would save them from their problems. The Jews have looked for their Messiah for thousands of years. The Christians look for a return of Christ to the earth and a thousand years of righteousness upon the earth. In reading the New Testament it is evident that the ancient apostles expected the return of Christ to be imminent. Many faiths of our modern age have predicted the return of Christ, and the leaders of these churches talk like it would be during their lifetimes. Dates have even been set for the "Rapture", many of which have come and gone. The most recent date of which I am aware is towards the end of the year 2011 when the Mayan Calendar ends and it marks an end of our age and some great new beginning, possibly the end of the world as we know it and the return of universal consciousness.

When talking about the dawn of the new age it is interesting to note that Christ taught, "But no one knows the date and hour when the end will be—not even the angels. No, nor even God's Son. Only the Father knows. The world will be at ease—banquets and parties and weddings—just as it was in Noah's time before the sudden coming of the flood; people wouldn't believe what was going to happen until the flood actually arrived and took them all away. So shall my coming be.

Two men will be working together in the fields, and one will be taken, the other left. Two women will be going about their household tasks; one will be taken, the other left.

So be prepared, for you don't know what day your Lord is coming." (Matthew 24:36-42)

Anyone who thinks they know when their Messiah will return is probably wrong. I think that one reason that no one really knows when the Millennium, the thousand years of peace upon the earth, will come is that it depends more upon the progress of the human race than upon some timeline of God's doing. As long as people, nations, families, and societies are willing to war and contend with each other we will have war, conflict, and misery here on earth. The whole world needs to be elevated to the position of being one with God. Everyone individually needs to become spiritually connected with God so that they are influenced by His spirit and come to realize that when they hurt anyone else they are only hurting themselves. We are all one with each other and one with God.

This cannot happen by force. God will not take away our ability to make choices. No authority, government, or religion can force a person to love their neighbor as themselves. This has to be a personal change that spreads all around the world, until "…no one then will need to speak to his friend or neighbor or brother, saying, "You, too, should know the Lord," because everyone, great and small, will know (Him) already." (Hebrews 8:11) The only way for a person to "know the Lord" is for him to personally connect spiritually with God.

Christ taught that there are really only two laws: love God and love others. He did not just say to love your family or friends, He taught to love everyone, saying, "…Love your enemies! Pray for those who persecute you!" (Matthew 5:44) When the world gets to the point that we love our enemies, we will try to help them instead of fight them. We will share with them our time, our wisdom, our worldly possessions, our oil, our technology; and the world will be in peace.

It is up to each human being to start now; we cannot wait for someone else to begin. Make peace with your spouse. Spend time with your children. Do something nice for the nasty neighbor down the street. We can all look around and find someone to help, some spirit to lift, some heart to heal. Do not expect anything in return, when another person is helped, everyone, including you, benefit. We are all one. We are all one with God. This is a very hard thing for people to remember and accept, but it is what we all need to live by in order to change the world and have peace finally come to earth.

CHAPTER VI
PERSONAL RESPONSIBILITY

1. We Choose

God has allowed us our freedom of choice here in this existence. The fact that we have freedom in no way absolves us of the consequences of our choices. I have read books and talked to others that maintain that there is no right or wrong. There is only what works and what does not work. We tend to make the best decision at the moment which will bring to us the most amount of perceived personal satisfaction.

We are a product of our choices. People in prison often admit that they are incarcerated because of the choices that they made in life. Often the path to prison starts with small choices which lead to others which eventually lead to a breaking of the laws of the land and incarceration. My choice to stay in college and finish my medical training allowed me to become a physician. We may have freedom of choice, but we have to live with the consequences of our choices. We not only make choices for ourselves but for our children and posterity and for all those for whom we have responsibility. The choices we make can have a great effect on ourselves and many other people. We need to be careful of the choices we make in life. Our choices reflect our true desires and beliefs. The universe provides us with what we truly desire.

God loves us. He wants us to by happy and joyful. He is all knowing and all loving. He gives us recommendations on how to live, not because of right or wrong, but He knows what works and what does not work. He knows what brings happiness and what brings misery. If we want to be happy it does not work to kill other people. It does work to treat them as ourselves. It does not work to seek after wealth to the exclusion of morality. It does work to seek first the Kingdom of God (personal spirituality) and then the spirit of God can inspire us in what we are supposed to be doing in our personal life and career.

Inasmuch as you keep my commandment you will prosper, (Deuteronomy 29:9) not because of some big reward from God, but because our personal relationship with the spirit allows us to create prosperity in our lives due to our personal thoughts, actions, and the universe responding to our personal power.

The message of ancient wisdom is that we can learn principles that, if followed, lead to peace and joy in our own lives and in the lives of those around us. The key to making the world a better place is to personally live the principles that lead to that. Principles are based on beliefs. If we believe that we are all one and one with God we will treat others like ourselves, because others are us and we are them and we are all one. Why would we ever hurt someone else if we really believed that we would just be hurting our self? It is the belief that we are separate from each other and that we are better than someone else that allows us to harm them. We think that our way is better than their way so we go to war to force them to be like us. It does not bring peace to think we are all separate. We need to realize that we are all one.

We are often given opportunities in our life which we may approach in a negative or positive way. Our approach to the opportunity is often what determines whether we will receive a blessing or a trial. For example when we are married we make a commitment to another person. That marriage may end in disaster and divorce, or it may bring much peace and joy throughout the years, depending on how the couple treat each other and work to overcome the problems and challenges in life. Some couples face difficulties and conflict by blaming and attacking each other. Other couples learn to truly become one with each other and work through problems with love, communication, compassion, and understanding. If someone wants the marriage to persist, they will make choices which support that desire. If someone acts in a negative manner in the marriage then they are telling the universe that they really do not value their marriage, they do not respect their partner, and they have a greater risk of divorce.

The Bible invites us to make a choice. "Decide today whom you will obey." (Joshua 24) Life is full of choices. It has been said that there are only two ways, the right way and the wrong way. We can choose to follow the inspirations of the spirit, or we can follow the passions of this world; the Spirit of God or the Ego. We may choose the path of light or the path of darkness. As a popular science-fiction film put it, we can choose the way of the Force, or we can choose the Dark Side. We can be part of our group or their group.

Life really is much more complex than the good versus evil paradigm. Every day, every moment of the day we are making choices, those choices form our life and determine all the various aspects of who we are. But, and this is important, no matter where we are on the path to happiness, no matter how many wrong choices we have made, right now we may make a better choice. There is always a better choice, and a best choice. The path to happiness and the path to misery are really the same path. It just depends on which way we are facing on that path. If we are miserable and suffering, we may, at any point, turn around and start making different or better choices. The road that goes up the hill is the same road that goes down the hill; it just depends on which way we are traveling. All of humanity is on that same road together. No one has to find a new road. All anyone has to do if they are not happy with where they are going is to turn around and start making better choices. The pain and suffering that we experience here on earth are provided to encourage everyone to make better choices. Our emotions are the best guide posts to the validity of our decisions and the direction of our life.

I was taught that wickedness never was happiness. What is wickedness? It is when we are doing things that are contrary to that spirit of inspiration within us. We are acting against our divine potential and our highest greatest good. We cannot impose our values on another person. What is wickedness for one may be proper for another. It all depends on where we are spiritually. Where our path in life is taking us and what our desires and goals are. The emotions of joy and sorrow are given us as guides to show us exactly what we should and should not be doing or thinking. If we are happy then we are in the spiritual flow and are progressing along our life path. When we are full of sorrow, depression, or despair we are missing our true potential in life and we need to change things in order to turn around on our path. Everyone's goals in life are different. This is why what makes me happy may make you sad. We cannot impose our personal goals on others.

Many people think that it is the materialism of the world that will bring them happiness and peace. They spend their entire lives developing their careers and chasing after money, fame, and power. The cable TV stations are filled with stories of the rich and famous and they often show their extravagant lifestyles. Many people watching seem to be jealous of the material wealth that these individuals have accumulated. The media depicts these people as smiling, happy, and comfortable. Our society is based currently on the motivation to acquire more things, cars, homes, wealth, power, and social position. The main purpose of the media, TV, and internet seems to be to make us desire more material things. If materialism truly brings happiness, then why do Americans, admittedly the wealthiest nation in recent history, have such a high rate of depression, violence, drug abuse, and divorce? We are becoming richer and our standard of living is increasing annually. So why is our rate of divorce and violence also increasing? It is a myth that materialism brings happiness. Just look around a little. Did money make the King of Rock and Roll or the King of Pop happier, wiser, and more emotionally balanced? Do Hollywood marriages really last? Does fame and power improve anyone's morals and family life? Does being elected President of the United States suddenly confer personal morality, integrity, or brilliance?

There is nothing basically wrong with having material possessions. In fact, I believe God wants us to have and acquire the things we want and need. It is not the material thing which causes our happiness or misery; it is the way we think, our attitude, which determines our mood. We are the only ones that can choose our thoughts. If we only think about the things of the world, money, fame, power, etc. then we will never be happy. These things do not confer happiness, they confer responsibility. We never really own anything. Ownership is an illusion of this earth life. When we acquire something, whether by purchasing, stealing, finding, or any other way, we become responsible for the care and maintenance of that object. We become the parent of the object and have to think about its needs. Some things need to be maintained, the oil needs to be changed in a car, or a house needs painting. Some things need to be cleaned, art objects need dusting, houses, cars, clothing all need cleaning. Landscaping needs to be watered, lawns mowed, shrubs trimmed, trees fertilized. Animals need attention, feeding, housing. Jewelry needs insurance, storage and cleaning. A career requires a lot of time and effort to maintain. Investments need to be monitored and maintained. The list goes on and on. The more things we have, the worse it becomes. Eventually, all we have time to think about are our material possessions. We become consumed with trying to maintain the "lifestyle to which we have become accustomed".

When all of our time and effort is spent on things, then our spirituality and our relationships with others suffer. The more time we spend thinking about our careers, our boats, our homes, the less time we have to think about God and our neighbors. The first two great commandments are to love God and love our neighbor. How can we love anyone if we do not have the time to spend thinking about them? Children feel this acutely, missing the affection and care which comes from having a loving parent thinking about them constantly. When parents try to substitute material things for true love and attention it cripples the children and perpetuates the worship of materialism. There are only 24 hours in a day, 1440 minutes or 86,400 seconds daily to use any way we desire. No one can control our thoughts, only we have the power to decide each second how we will best use our greatest resource, our minds.

I know about these things from personal experience. I married at a fairly young age and had three children before I even graduated from medical school. We lived on loans and what income came from meager part time jobs. We had nothing really, I rode a bicycle to school, and we rented an older apartment in a poor area of town. I have great memories of that era, taking the kids to the park and playing on the swings, going for walks, and watching the sunset. I built some of our furniture with simple hand tools and I was proud of the simple pieces I produced with my own hands. I enjoyed gardening and planted flowers and vegetables in the yard.

Years later I had it all. I was a successful physician, with my own medical office, employing other physicians and a staff of fifteen other people. I was well respected in my community and had responsibilities at my church. I had a huge brick house with large white columns out front on a few acres of land. I had a pool in the back yard, a big garage filled with fancy woodworking tools, and lots of shiny new cars. I spent my whole time maintaining what I had. The insurance on the cars and home and the medical malpractice required a large amount of cash for which I had to work. I had to hire gardeners because I did not have time anymore to work in the yard. I had problems with depression and anxiety because I always felt overextended and guilty about the things I neglected.

The forces of the universe seem to have a way of giving us exactly what we really want, not what we think we want. First my business partner of ten years decided it was time to leave and find new associations, many of our employees left with her. I went through a year of revamping my business and hiring new employees and spent precious resources buying her out of her share of the business. Then next year I found out that my wife of twenty years was seeing another man and she wanted a divorce. She had not loved me for years and she wanted to marry another man. I reacted irresponsibly by becoming involved with the party scene, carousing with friends frequently until late at night. My business floundered and I struggled both spiritually and materially. Eventually my anxiety and depression worsened and I went to a psychiatrist who started me on a myriad of medications which resulted in a severe car accident. I was left permanently disabled, unable to run my business. The business went bankrupt, I lost everything I had worked so hard to obtain, my family, my career, my health, and my possessions.

At that time I truly found out what was important in my life. I found out that I was loved. My current wife stayed with me through this disaster. My parents and siblings still stood by me. I found out that I could be happy without all the toys I had once desired. Over the next few years I established a new equilibrium in which I had much less, much less responsibility and much fewer material possessions. I found myself much happier in this new state, and I am glad that I went through these reversals of life. I found out that the stuff that did not really matter fell away, and that which I really valued continued in my life.

Often times we have to go through a purging process in life to be able to see who we really are and what we really desire. Sometimes it is forced upon us and sometimes it is by choice. I believe that change is always for the good. It is the universe responding to our true thoughts and desires. We need to be very careful what we want, because the universe will give us exactly what we truly desire. Sometimes we look around and see the wealth and fancy lifestyles of others and we become jealous. If we really knew what it took to achieve and maintain such a lifestyle we would realize that our attempt to attain it would make us miserable. If we really wanted the fame and fortune we would have it already, or we would be working hard to obtain it. If the lifestyle does not truly fit who we are deep down inside, then that lifestyle is not for us. I am happier now pulling weeds in my own small backyard than I ever was when I hired gardeners to keep my estate in perfect splendor.

2. Control Thoughts

We humans are capable of much more that what most people realize. The media is filled with stories of extra sensory perception, telekinesis, telepathy and other mysterious powers and perceptions. The pop culture and media suggestions are more accurate than we think. Christ taught in the New Testament that we have the ability to perform many "miracles" and that we should emulate Him. He taught the truth that we have supernatural powers which each and every one of us may develop though our own efforts to grow and mature spiritually. He invites us to follow Him. We have to remember that two people have walked on water. When Christ walked on water, He invited Peter to walk on water with Him. Christ invites us to "walk with Him" also. When Peter became afraid and started to sink in the waters, Christ chastised him with the words, "O man of little faith. Why did you doubt me?" (Matthew 14:31)

Doubt prevents belief. What we believe is what happens. This is directly related to the way the universe responds to our thoughts. What we think about creates electrical signals which propagate out into the universe. The universe always responds to our thoughts and we will experience the results of that response. If our thoughts are positive, positive things will happen to us and around us. If our thoughts are negative, negativity in our life will result. Most of us do not recognize this direct connection. We often believe that we are powerless in the universe and have no control over our own lives and destiny. Nothing could be further than the truth. We are the creators of our own futures. Every moment of every day we are thinking things and doing things. These thoughts and actions create our futures. We can do anything that we believe we can do. It is the fear and doubt that often occurs within us that prevents us from being successful in our plans. Fear prevents belief.

Edgar Cayce often stated while in the trance state that "mind is the builder". This is very accurate. Our minds create thoughts. The thoughts create actions. The actions create our futures. It is more that this also. It is too simplistic to view our thoughts as leading to our personal decisions and actions. Our thoughts also spread out into the universe and affect everything around us and even the actions of others. When someone is afraid, that fear is read by animals and other people increasing the risk of attack to that fearful person. The fear is not a just a response to the danger present, but actually creates the danger. If that person was able to be calm in a similar circumstance the risk of danger would be substantially lessened. We are in control of our thoughts. No one can tell us what to think. No one can force us to think a certain way. Only we can decide what to keep in our minds and what to reject. We then are ultimately in control of out own lives and our own future, because only we can control our thoughts. What we think about day to day will determine our future.

Some people do not like the idea that they are in control of their lives. They would like to think that others are the cause of their problems and they like to blame others for negative events in their lives. This blaming tendency impairs one's ability to overcome problems. Until we take responsibility for our life and its associated problems we cannot really do anything to change the situation. If we are blaming others we are giving those people control over our life. We give away our personal power to those who we blame for our problems. In actuality, we are the only ones who are in control of our own life. Every detail of our life is a direct expression of the thoughts and decisions we have made. Some of these decisions occurred even before we were born here into this present life on this earth. We had much to say about where, when, and by whom we would be born. When we have the big picture about our eternal nature and the reasons we were born here on this earth at this time, we will realize that all the events we perceive as problems in our life are only opportunities to grow and develop further towards perfection.

We each need to look at the reasons we act. We should be motivated by love for the Lord and his children and not for gain, glory, or other less worthy objectives. We need to emulate the Savior when dealing with others we encounter in this earth life.

The New Testament tells of Christ's interaction with an adulterous woman. "Jesus returned to the Mount of Olives, but early the next morning he was back again at the Temple. A crowd soon gathered, and he sat down and talked to them. As he was speaking, the Jewish leaders and Pharisees brought a woman caught in adultery and placed her out in front of the staring crowd.

"Teacher," they said to Jesus, "this woman was caught in the very act of adultery. Moses' law says to kill her. What about it?"

They were trying to trap him into saying something they could use against him, but Jesus stooped down and wrote in the dust with his finger. They kept demanding and answer, so he stood up again and said, "All right, hurl the stones at her until she dies. But only he who never sinned may throw the first!"

Then he stooped down again and wrote some more in the dust. And the Jewish leaders slipped away one by one, beginning with the eldest, until only Jesus was left in front of the crowd with the woman.

Then Jesus stood up again and said to her, "Where are your accusers? Didn't even one of them condemn you?"

"No, sir," she said.

And Jesus said, "Neither do I. Go and sin no more."" (John 8:1-11)

Are we part of the group of people with the stones to throw at the woman taken in unlawful actions or are we, like Christ, diffusing the situation with forgiveness, love, and patience, asking only "Woman, where are your accusers? Go and sin no more."

The way we act when we brush up against those strangers around us really tells us a lot about our spiritual progression. In traffic are we annoyed by the slow poke in front of us or are we yelling at the guy that cut us off? We cannot take the actions of others personally. Someone may do something which is annoying but we can forgive and choose not to be annoyed. We always have our choice in what to believe, how to think personally, and how to respond to others' behavior.

I know a man who recently got a job as a waiter at a local restaurant. He was supposed to know the menu backwards and forwards and was given training and time to study the information. Prior to commencing his job, he was given a test about the menu. He missed ten questions out of one hundred and twenty. He was quizzed orally on the points he missed until he knew the answers well. After his first day working his manager made him retake the exam. The man was able to get all the questions right. I talked to that man after this experience and was surprised to find him upset about the retesting. He thought that since he had done so well on the initial exam, the manager should have praised him instead of retesting him. He was angry at the manager and thought of ways to get revenge and irritate the manager. I tried to help this man understand that the manager probably required all the employees to know the complete menu without error. I pointed out that the manager was just fulfilling the requirements of his job and was not out to get my friend personally. My friend took this interaction way too personally.

We each have the opportunity to react in any way we desire to the actions of others. Most of us take things too personally and get worked up over innocent actions. We would live in a better world if people would be quicker to see the good in others and slower to judge them.

In 1845, the Franklin expedition set sail in two ships from England in search of a northwest passage through the Arctic to the Pacific Ocean. Each sailing vessel contained a backup steam engine and enough coal for the ship to run on auxiliary power for twelve days— that was in preparation for a voyage that was expected to take up to three years. Apparently, rather than storing extra coal, they brought along provisions for their own immediate comfort. Included on board were a hand organ, china place settings, wine glasses, and ornate sterling silverware with large, solid handles engraved with the officers' initials and family crests.

None of the 138 men returned alive. Instead, their remains were later discovered at various places across the frozen Arctic. One group from the Franklin expedition had apparently taken off in search of civilization. There among the frozen bodies, among those men who were desperately hiking through life-threatening conditions for their survival, was the heavy, engraved silverware they had been hauling across the frozen wasteland.

Many of us tend to act in a manner similar to the men of this failed expedition. We worry too much about the material things of this world which do not bring any lasting happiness or joy and we ignore many of the spiritual things that are crucial to our emotional stability and our eternal survival. We need to be willing to put aside the pursuit of extravagance for the pursuit of spirituality. We need to know when it is more important to pack coal for our trip and when we can be frivolous and bring silverware and wine glasses.

Christ teaches this principle when he told the parable of the ten bridesmaids. "The Kingdom of Heaven can be illustrated by the story of ten bridesmaids who took their lamps and went to meet the bridegroom. But only five of them were wise enough to fill their lamps with oil, while the other five were foolish and forgot.

So when the bridegroom was delayed, they lay down to rest until midnight, when they were roused by the shout, "The bridegroom is coming! Come out and welcome him!"

All the girls jumped up and trimmed their lamps. Then the five who hadn't any oil begged the others to share with them, for their lamps were going out.

But the others replied, "We haven't enough. Go instead to the shops and buy some for yourselves."

But while they were gone, the bridegroom came, and those who were ready went in with him to the marriage feast, and the door was locked.

Later, when the other five returned they stood outside, calling, "Sir, open the door for us!"

But he called back, "Go away! It is too late!"

So stay awake and be prepared, for you do not know the date or moment of my return." (Matthew 25:1-13)

The five foolish bridesmaids were neglectful in their preparations and did not provide enough of the essential oil for the situation. The five wise bridesmaids were well prepared for every contingency, including a long delay in the arrival of the wedding party. We have to ask, what is the essential oil in our own lives? I believe that it is the personal relationship that we develop during our lives with God. This relationship cannot be bought; it cannot be borrowed or shared. It is just as available to the rich and to the poor, to the healthy and to the infirm. No matter where we live or what our condition in life, a spiritual relationship with God is readily available to all humanity. Our own connection to deity is our own responsibility and our own doing. It must be developed over time with a consistent desire to know God and seek out His Spirit through study, prayer, meditation, and love.

We do things for Love, Duty, or Fear. Love is I want to, Duty is I have to, Fear is I better do it or else. Hell fire and damnation may encourage many people to live in a particular way, but it is much better when people perform actions due to a sense of love. Love for God, love for others, love for ourselves. It is only acting through love that we strengthen our connection to God and those around us. We may go through the motions of religious ritual or community service, but unless those motions are based on love we are really not fulfilling our potential. People can pretty much tell if we are going through the motions on their behalf or if we truly have a loving concern for them. God knows our thoughts and the reasons for our actions and we are not about to fool Him into thinking our actions are based on love if they are otherwise.

We have to be honest with ourselves. Abraham Lincoln said, "When I do good I feel good, when I do bad I feel bad." Each moment of each day we need to observe the pattern of our thoughts. Are we acting out of love of our fellow man? Are we performing out of fear? Do we feel good? If we are thinking and acting according to our highest potential, we will be filled with joy and happiness. There is no need to suffer for righteousness. Doing well and serving others only brings a feeling of joy.

3. Personal Spirituality

If God had a message for you, would you be able to get it? Do you spend enough time each day meditating, praying and being in tune with the spirit of God to receive the message? Each of us has the ability to communicate with God and to ask Him what is right for us. If we are not working to develop ourselves spiritually then we are not realizing our full potential as human beings. Going through the motions of religious rituals and Sunday meetings does not count much for personal spirituality. It is our own responsibility to seek out the divine spirit which permeates the universe. We cannot abrogate this important task to another.

Throughout my training and my career as a medical doctor I was constantly exposed to scientific information and descriptions which pretty much left any concept of God or spirituality out of the subject. When in medical school making clinical hospital rounds with the teaching physician, if I were asked why I believed a patient had a certain disease it would always be better for me to state the signs and symptoms and pathophysiology which lead to the logical suggestion of possible diagnoses. It was never appropriate to answer that my feelings of intuition suggested a specific diagnosis. Lab tests, diagnostic procedures, and proposed treatments would all follow accepted protocols and decision algorithms as specified by the current medical standards. Medical practice was based on standards of the medical community and was not subject to personal inspiration from deity.

I attained a personal connection with the divine long before I ever went to medical school. One of the great motivators for my interest in becoming a physician in the first place came from an epiphany I had while I was in college. At the time I was much more interested in mechanical things, cars, airplanes, robots, etc. and I worked as a car mechanic during high school. I had a knack for figuring out how things work, what was wrong with them, and how to fix them. I could fix just about anything mechanical. I spent much of my childhood building airplane and car models, working on bicycles, and helping my father with car maintenance. In college I had intended to become an engineer like my father and several brothers. I thought I would work in mechanical engineering designing cars or jets for a living.

In October 1977 I read a magazine article during an airplane trip about a new medical specialty, family practice. While reading about the aspects defining this new breed of doctor, one who specialized in the whole person, a generalist with more training and certification than the old fashioned general practitioner of my childhood, I received a strong spiritual sensation and a very strong thought that I should pursue a career in this new field. This was a bolt of inspiration from the source I consider to be divine. Based on this experience, I changed my direction in life and applied to medical school. I was accepted to the University of Arizona Medical School and graduated in 1985. I completed my family practice specialty training in 1988.

Before ever stepping foot in medical school, I had already developed a relationship with God. I had learned to trust the intuitive feelings of spirituality, even to the point of changing my intended career from engineering to medicine. I trusted that sense of inspiration more than any other influence in my life. This made medical school very interesting for me. Some of the things taught in medical school did not seem "true" to me in the spiritual sense. ("It is impossible for a woman to feel her fetus before sixteen weeks gestation, any sensation she has is just intestinal gas.") I often could use intuition to reach a conclusion about a patient, or "feel" when I should order certain lab tests or perform certain examinations. When making rounds with other students and the attending physician, I often "knew" whether a student gave a correct answer or not. ("Well Doctor Robertson, what do you think of the analysis by Doctor Smith?" "Doctor Smith is wrong; the patient has pericarditis, not congestive heart disease.") Later, I used my intuition to guide my treatment of patients in my medical practice. ("Let us order a brain MRI. Your dizziness seems more worrisome than normal" and the results show a brain tumor. Or, "We should biopsy that small mole", and it is early melanoma.) My sense of intuition became so strong over the years that I could "feel" what was wrong with a patient when I picked up their medical chart and entered the exam room. I was always glad that I followed the insights that were whispered to me through that sense of knowledge that I developed and learned to trust.

Scientists and anthropologists have often explained the sensations which I value as spiritual as random electrical or chemical activity in the nervous system. They cite examples of disease states which are clearly not spiritual and are extremely debilitating to the patient's ability to function in society. For example, schizophrenia is a disease where, among other things, the patient hears voices that are not present, has trouble distinguishing between fantasy and reality, and experiences disordered thought processes. People with schizophenia are often fanatically religious. Some scientists theorize that religious doctrine and beliefs were originally started by this type of person, someone who believes himself to be the son of God, hears Gods voice from a burning bush, sees the dead come back to life, wrestles with angels and devils, and teaches that mankind is wicked and needs to appease God's wrath. Patients with obsessive compulsive disease have their life intruded on by the irresistible urge to perform some behavior over and over again. They are often obsessed with cleanliness, checking on things, counting, and magical numbers. A strong similarity between the rituals and requirements of many ancient religions and the repetitive patterns of OCD has long been noted by scientists. Speculation exists that these religious requirements were first started by members of the religious community who suffered with OCD. For example, the well known Christian reformer, Martin Luther, showed evidence of OCD in his journal writing. Sigmund Freud made the link in his 1907 essay "Obsessive Acts and Religious Practices" describing "religion as a universal obsessional neurosis." Science tells us that my sensations of inspiration and my need to have order in my life are just milder manifestations of the same traits. Mental health is a continuum, there is no disease or disorder in my case while in a severe form the same tendencies are very debilitating and considered mental illness.

Descriptions of these ideas are accessible in an insightful book, *"The Trouble With Testosterone and Other Essays on the Biology of the Human Predicament"* by Robert M. Sapolsky. Dr. Sapolsky is a professor of biology and neuroscience at Stanford University. He makes the point that the genetic traits for some of these severe mental health disorders exist in the gene pool because the tendencies for these behaviors confer a survival advantage. All organisms adapt to their environment and as a species the traits that provide a reproductive advantage eventually permeate the entire species, this is the principle of natural selection. He maintains that the genetic advantage which keeps these traits in the gene pool is from the honor conferred on people manifesting a mild form of these traits in society. Religious people are more likely to become the medicine men, the clergy, the respected, and are therefore more likely to have food in times of famine, more material security, and more opportunity to reproduce, so eventually the traits providing for religious experience spread through the gene pool.

I believe that the ability to be sensitive to the unseen forces of the universe conveys a genetic advantage in and of itself. Just like the ability to translate the mechanical vibrations in the air to a sensation of sound in the brain (ie. hearing) is advantageous to the survival of the human species, I think that the ability to perceive the energy forces in the universe as a sensation or feeling in the mind is very advantageous. If two primitive men were out hunting, and one felt danger and went back to the village, and the other ignored or did not feel the sensation of danger and was killed, the one escaping the danger would live to reproduce and teach others to pay attention to that feeling. Whatever name we use, the spirit of God, the zero point field, the energy flux of life, this force that spreads through the universe is real. The ability to be sensitive to this force and learn wisdom and truth from it is important.

The fact that scientists often do not believe that the spiritual force exists, either because they are genetically not able to feel it, or they discount the experience as being imaginary and ignore it, does not make the existence of the force less real. Gravity existed even before scientists were aware of it. Many things that we were sure of years ago have been disproved, the world is not the center of the universe, the world is not flat, and we are not alone in the universe. We are actually all one, and we are one with God.

Obviously, my interpretation of these phenomena is different from mainstream scientific interpretation. That is the beauty of life. We can all have our own personal opinions and ideas and lifestyles.

Diversity is essential in a healthy society. I have no need to try to force a skeptic to believe that I am right and that he is wrong any more than he has a need to force me to believe he is right and I am wrong. Right and wrong really are immaterial and traditionally such arguments have only led to violence and bloodshed. Too much bloodshed and suffering occurs because of nations and individuals squabbling about who is right. It really does not make any difference anyway. Everyone has their own ability to choose for themselves what they want to believe.

Everyone believes something. Whether we put our belief system on the secular, the scientific, or the metaphysical we all choose some belief system. We each choose our personal involvement with spirituality and religious ritual. We can be totally atheistic, agnostic, traditional, fanatical, or any combination of belief and activity in a church that we desire. We have a personal need to be anchored in some basic belief system. Spirituality is not the same thing as religiosity. Personal spirituality is a person's personal relationship with and understanding of God. Many religions and churches exist on the earth and each of us must make a choice on what to believe and follow. I believe that many religions are based on a smattering of truth joined with the philosophies of the world. I believe that God does reveal truth to humans so that we can live in more peace, comfort, and grow and mature spiritually. God does not force anyone to believe like anyone else, and we here on this earth should not try to force anyone to believe like we do. We have had too many wars and too much bloodshed by people who used religious differences as a basis for killing others. Each of us has our own connection with God and as we progress spiritually, this connection should become stronger. We need to listen to our hearts. The spirit of God within each of us will guide us and help us to decide what is true for ourselves. We need to hear the voice of the spirit of truth louder that the noise of our fellow humans. We can tell others about our personal beliefs, but we should never force or coerce others to our point of view. Let God do the arguing for Himself. He is All Powerful, if there is some all important truth that we all must know, He will reveal it.

All the arguments, all the philosophies, all the religions can be boiled down to this: what is my relationship with God? The beauty of this is that any one of us may perform the steps necessary to open the lines of communication with God and find out for ourselves. We do not have to rely on anyone else than God Himself for this answer. Our relationship with deity is our responsibility. It is not up to our parents, our teachers, our pastors, or our lovers to make us believe something. It is up to us and up to God. If God wants us to believe in a certain way then He can tell us about it. We are the only ones who can make ourselves more spiritually minded.

Faith, hope, and charity are three things which are essential for those seeking greater spiritual knowledge. They seem to always be talked about in the same order, first faith, then hope, and finally charity. I believe that this teaches a natural progression in a person's spiritual development. Faith has to come first. Without faith there is really no motivation for delving further into spiritual learning. A person must have faith in something prior to any action on his part. If a farmer does not have faith that he can harvest a crop he will never prepare the soil, waste money on buying seed, or spend the time planting and tending the crops. Faith precedes his action; it is the motivator, the determination to succeed at any goal. Would anyone invest in the stock market if they did not believe that they would have a reasonable return on their money? Would anyone go to work if they did not think that they would be successful and be able to earn some amount of income? Faith is the first principle of action. Without faith there is nothing.

In Hebrews chapter 11 Paul tells about faith and how it is the basis for action. He relates it to working miracles, but faith is in action with almost anything which we accomplish during our lives here. He states, "What is faith? It is the confident assurance that something we want is going to happen. It is the certainty that what we hope for is waiting for us, even though we cannot see it up ahead." (Hebrews 11:1)

Faith can only really exist when we believe in something which is real. We may believe that when we plant pebbles in the soil a great money tree will spring forth, but our belief is not faith, and the money tree will never blossom. Faith grows through our experience. We learn what things in which to really believe and what things are merely our childish imaginations. Sometimes the things we were taught as children to be true we find to be myths as we grow older. For instance, many of us believed in Santa Clause in our youth. We were told by those in authority that he existed and the evidence of our belief came every year on December 25th. When we found out that our parents had deceived us it may have been hard to accept at first, but most adults have adjusted to the idea that Santa is a fun tradition, but not a real being. Some adults feel the same way about God. They feel that the things they were told about God in their youth no longer seem to correlate with their observation of truth and reality, and so they reject the concept of a loving supreme being as just another tradition of their ancestors.

Spiritual truth may be tested and experimented with just like any truth. Truth is no respecter of persons. Anyone seeking truth may find it. Scientific truth may be discovered through scientific experimentation. Who ever does the experiment will be able to verify the truth being tested. If a person wants to test what grows when planted, he only needs to plant some seeds and compare the results with planting some pebbles. Under the right conditions the seeds will sprout for whoever conducts the experiment. Faith is the same way; the way to test spiritual truth is through spiritual means. One has to have an open mind to the possibility of success and one has to have a sincere desire to conduct the experiment. If the person experimenting with the seeds is so agnostic that he neglects to water the seeds, the experiment will fail, thus confirming to him the validity of his doubt.

The easiest way for a person to find out for himself if God really exists is to personally perform the experiment that the teachers of religion have recommended throughout all of humanity. It is very basic, all you have to do is to start reading and studying scripture, start living according to your conscience, and start praying and meditating. Most importantly we have to develop a real desire to know. It seems strange to some people that they need to pray to find out that God exists, but God is the only one who can communicate His existence to anyone. I cannot prove God exists, but He can. He will. He is all powerful and He desires to communicate with each one of us. I know without any doubt that if we will put aside our pride and Ego, our prejudice and traditions, and conduct the experiment, God will make Himself known to each of us. We must be persistent; God will answer when it is in our best interest to know Him. If we are not yet ready for the spiritual insight we will not receive the knowledge. We have to be willing and ready to change our opinions and our behaviors before God will provide us with new information. It may be hard to work through this type of experiment, but it is worth all the struggle and effort that we put into it. It is worth developing a knowledge and relationship with deity. Each of us can only benefit from the experience and every part of our life, our work, our family relationships, and our self esteem will all improve. Faith is the first step. We cannot place the cart before the horse. A firm knowledge of God and a communication from Him directly will be a cherished gift. Direct communication from God will be like a spring of living water from which we may drink every day throughout our life. Christ invited Peter to walk on water. Christ invites each of us to follow Him. We can while we have faith. All things are possible to us if we are close enough to the spirit of God. Christ told His disciples, "In solemn truth I tell you, anyone believing in me shall do the same miracles I have done, and even greater ones." (John 14:12)

We have been told to have faith like a mustard seed. When asked by his disciple why they could not perform a miracle, Christ told them "Because of your little faith. For if you had faith even as small as a tiny mustard seed you could say to this mountain, "Move!" and it would go far away. Nothing would be impossible." (Matthew 17:20)

The mustard seed is full of symbolism. The obvious symbol refers to the size of the seed. It is a very tiny seed, yet the mustard plant is one of the largest of the herbs. The analogy that from very small beginnings great power may be manifested is well known. When I think about the seed, I realize that there is more to it than the size of the seed. I remember that a seed may survive the worst drought, one which may destroy living plants and even entire forests. The seed remains dormant until conditions are right for the growth of the plant. The desert springs forth with plants and flowers after a few good rainstorms. The flowers appear in the spring after the snow thaws. The seeds wait patiently and then burst forth with activity when the time is right. The same must be true for us. We need to be patient and wait until conditions are right to receive the spiritual manifestation we seek. We can manifest many miracles when we put ourselves in harmony with the universe and the ways of God. With the experience we gain from following our spiritual pathway we achieve increased faith and wisdom. Our faith grows and grows as we become closer and closer to the divine ideal.

The next step in the progression in spiritual development is to gain hope in a better future. Hope for an improved life here on earth and a better afterlife comes directly from knowledge of God's existence and assurance that He has a loving interest in each of us personally. As we develop faith we also develop hope. When our faith grows, our communication with God increases, and our spiritual knowledge increases also. The more we begin to understand, the more we begin to understand and appreciate our relationship with God. Understanding who we are in relationship to God allows us to have hope that God does know who we are and loves us individually.

Once we are secure with our relationship with God we naturally have increased capacity for divine love. Charity is divine love. Divine love is God's love. Divine love comes from our relationship with God. The influence of God's spirit in our life inspires us to greater capacity to love others, to feel, to think, and to act in accord with God's perspective. We begin to realize that we really are all one and we are one with God. We have desires for others to find the happiness and joy that we feel when we are spiritually connected. We know that by helping others in their life we will only be happier ourselves. The two commandments, love God and love others become part of our nature. We no longer have to argue with our spouse because we are one with them. We no longer have to dodge our boss, because we are one with him and we love our job. We do not have to worry about rude drivers cutting in front, because we are one with them. We no longer ignore our children because we are one with them. We spend our time thinking the world is a wonderful place, because we are one with the world. We finally become one with God and our love for God and our fellow man motivates our actions. Instead of fear or duty being the basis of our action, we start acting out of love.

CONCLUSION

Years ago, I attended a very ill patient named Jim who was about fifty years old. He had a severe pneumonia for which I placed him in the intensive care unit (ICU) of the hospital. All day long I watched over him, seeing him go rapidly downhill. I consulted a myriad of specialists to help me with his care. At the end of the first day in the ICU his respiratory system, cardiac system, nervous system, and renal system were all failing. He was hooked up to every life support machine possible and alarms kept going off due to his instability. He was about to die. I knew it, his spouse knew it, the nursing staff knew it, and the specialists knew it. There was little hope of him being alive the next morning. That night I laid in bed exhausted, going over in my mind all that we had done for Jim. I kept asking myself if there was anything I was missing in his care, something that I could do to improve Jim's condition. It was after midnight, while meditating, that the spirit whispered in my mind that I should go and administer to Jim by "laying on of hands." I rationalized for a while why I should not get up out of my bed in the middle of the night, but the voice of God within me was insistent and emphatic. If I did not go right then, Jim would die that night.

I got out of bed and called a local pastor that I knew to go with me. We got to Jim's bedside at about 2:00 AM. Jim's blood pressure was dropping and his heart was skipping beats. The pastor said a prayer and then we both laid our hands on Jim's head and I prayed a blessing upon him. During my blessing I had the distinct impression that Jim's spirit had left his body and that he was hovering near the ceiling in the room watching us. I commanded by the name of Jesus Christ and by the power of the priesthood which we held, that Jim's spirit re-enter his body and stay there until his body could heal. The body jerked suddenly at my pronouncement and the blood pressure and heart monitors stabilized. The machines' warning alarms stopped. I felt joyful and hopeful inside, knowing that Jim would now live.

Jim recovered completely. He had sustained a stroke, but his brain recovered without any mental loss. His lungs recovered and he could breathe air without a respirator. His heart sustained a severe heart attack, but recovered without any impairment. All of his internal organs that were damaged healed completely. Jim walked out of the hospital two months later. Jim remained in my practice for several years. He had a complete recovery and resumed his normal career and lifestyle. He out lived his spouse. I have lost contact with Jim, but I know that a miracle occurred on the night that I commanded his spirit to return to his body.

I personally have performed many miracles during my life. I know that we are the masters of our lives and that we can accomplish anything in our lives that we desire. I am no one special. I know that we are all capable of performing miracles. We just need to connect with God spiritually and have a little faith. We are truly all one and we are one with God. As one we may create a life of joy and a world of peace.

SUGGESTED READING

Brown, Sylvia, *God, Creation, and Tools for Life,* Hay House, Inc., 2000.

Browne, Sylvia, *Soul's Perfection,* Hay House, Inc., 2000.

Calleman, Carl Johan, Ph.D., *The Mayan Calendar and the Transformation of Consciousness,* Bear & Company, 2004.

McArthur, Bruce, *Your Life: Why It Is the Way It Is and What You Can Do About It—Understanding the Universal Laws,* ARE Press, 1993.

McTaggart, Lynn, *The Field The Quest for the Secret Force of the Universe,* HarperCollins Publishers Inc., 2002.

Newton, Michael, Ph.D., *Journey of Souls: Case Studies of Life Between Lives,* Llewellyn Publications, 1994.

Newton, Michael, Ph.D., *Destiny of Souls: New Case Studies of Life Between Lives,* Llewellyn Publications, 2004.

Renard, Gary R., *The Disappearance of the Universe,* Hay House, Inc., 2004.

Roberts, Jane, *Seth Speaks, The Eternal Validity of the Soul,* Amber—Allen Publishing, 1994.

Ruiz, Don Miguel, *The Four Agreements: A practical guide to personal freedom,* Amber-Allen Publishing, Inc., 1997

Sargeant, Winthrop, Translator, *The Bhagavad Gita,* State University of New York Press, 1994.

Sugrue, Thomas, *Story of Edgar Cayce: There is a River,* ARE Press, 1997.

Tarnas, Richard, *The Passion of the Western Mind Understanding the Ideas That Have Shaped Our World View,* Ballantine Books, 1991.

The Living Bible, Tyndale House Publishers, Inc., 1971.

Walsch, Neale Donald, *Conversations with God: an uncommon dialogue,* G.P. Putnam's Sons, 1996.

Walsch, Neale Donald, *The new Revelations: A conversation with God,* ATRIA Books, 2002.

Walsch, Neale Donald, *What God Wants A compelling Answer to Humanity's Biggest Question,* ATRIA Books, 2005.

Ward, Paul Von, *Gods, Genes, and Consciousness: Nonhuman intervention in human history,* Hampton Roads Publishing Company, Inc., 2004.

Printed in the United States
59511LVS00002B/163-210